Eduqas **GCSE**

Food Preparation and Nutrition

Revision Guide

Jayne Hill

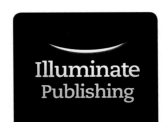

Illuminate Publishing

Published in 2017 by Illuminate Publishing Ltd, PO Box 1160,
Cheltenham, Gloucestershire GL50 9RW

Orders: Please visit www.illuminatepublishisng.com

or email sales@illuminatepublishing.com

British Library Cataloguing-in-Publication Data

A catalogue record for this book is available from the British Library.

ISBN 978-1-908682-87-1

Printed by Cambrian Printers, Aberystwyth

07.19

The publishers' policy is to use papers that are natural, renewable and recyclable products made
from wood grown in sustainable forests. The logging and manufacturing processes are expected
to conform to the environmental regulations of the country of origin.

Every effort has been made to contact copyright holders of material produced in this book.
Great care has been taken by the author and publishers to ensure that either formal permission has
been granted for the use of copyright material reproduced, or that copyright material has been used
under the provision of fair-dealing guidelines in the UK – specifically that it has been used sparingly,
solely for the purpose of criticism and review, and has been properly acknowledged. If notified,
the publisher will be pleased to rectify any errors or omissions at the earliest opportunity.

This material has been endorsed by WJEC Eduqas and offers high-quality support for the delivery
of Eduqas qualifications. While this material has been through an Eduqas quality assurance
process, all responsibility for content remains with the publisher.

Editor: Dawn Booth

Design and layout: emc design ltd

Cover photograph: Stolyevych Yuliya

CONTENTS

First off, I really hope you find this book helpful with your revision!

Food Preparation and Nutrition is a huge subject, so I decided this revision guide needs to focus on the 'bare-bones' of the course. I've used my knowledge gained from teaching and examining this subject area to guide you towards exam success.

You might wonder what the best way to use this guide is. Well, how about using it alongside your weekly lessons and homework – read the relevant revision guide chapter BEFORE you start each new topic, so that you arrive at the lesson with a bit of knowledge in hand!

Also, use it to get the best grade you can. To do well you must understand exactly what each question asks and show the examiner precisely what you know. Put simply, if you are aiming at grade 4/5 you'll need to learn the facts from each chapter and use them in answering extended writing questions. For those of you with either grade 8 or grade 9 targets you must learn the facts as well as be able to write about them in much more detail.

What does this guide contain?

1. The chapters follow the structure of the main textbook, which follows the structure of your GCSE specification. When revising a topic – say 'Dairy foods' – jot down and learn all the key words and phrases in the guide. If there's something you don't understand, look it up in the main textbook.

2. You'll find mind maps at the start of each chapter to highlight key phrases or sub-topics that need learning. These are a great way of giving you a skeleton of information. Once you have the basic skeleton clear in your mind, build up further knowledge onto each of the mind map's branches.

3. 'Quickfire' questions pop up regularly and are short and snappy: you should be able to quickly recall the answers. Use them to test yourself as you go along. 'Grade boosts' are designed for you to extend subject knowledge and help you write more detailed answers.

4. Finally, I suggest you **DO NOT** leave revision until the night before the exam! I'm a teacher and of course I would say this … but it's true! Doing well in the exam comes as the end result of a planned revision strategy, so make this book a central part of that.

What makes revision effective?

In school you will start revising for the GCSE long before the actual exam day. Use this time wisely and make each lesson count.

Have a revision plan for the subject and all the key topics, then break your learning into small chunks of time. It's proven that most people can't sit for hours at a stretch revising well.

Revise for 20–30 minutes on a topic. Time yourself if necessary. When time's up, review and revisit what you've looked at before taking a ten-minute break. Then begin another 20–30 minute revision session.

Use any 'spare' time you can. For example, use the ten minutes during tutor time, or five minutes at break time, or ten minutes while waiting for your bus. In each of those short revision times you can learn **one fact** from the book, such as the five main nutrients or learn how to **explain one** scientific principle/nutrient.

Try to teach what you know to a friend or family member. Getting someone to ask you questions on what you've just revised is probably one of the best ways to learn and understand a topic.

Mind map each topic using different-coloured pens – this is great for visual learners.

Record yourself, then keep listening to it – great for aural learners.

Write key words and the most important facts from each chapter onto revision cards. Then keep reading these cards until you know them off by heart – you have now learned the facts.

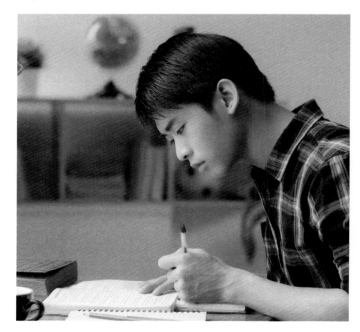

While you might be able to recall and list facts, this is only part of what you need in order to shine in the exam. Can you **explain** these facts? Do you understand what they mean and how they're done? Read on and find out ...

A question beginning '**Explain**' or '**Describe**' or '**Discuss**' or '**Evaluate**' means you have to extend the points made using 'PEE', which stands for **POINT EXPLAIN EXAMPLE**. You need to make your **point**, then **explain** that point to show you understand it and, where possible, give examples.

Let's apply that to a typical Food and Nutrition type question, which is colour-coded so that you can see the rules we just looked at in PEE:

> Can you see that we've colour-coded these words?

QUESTION

'Explain why protein is important in the diet.'

A BASIC ANSWER:

Protein is needed for growth and repair and is found in meat.

> And we've colour-coded both these answers here!

AN ADVANCED ANSWER:

Protein is needed for growth, repair and maintenance of cells, and is classified into high and low biological value (HBV and LVB) proteins. HBV proteins contain all the essential amino acids the body needs, whereas LBV proteins are missing one or more essential amino acids. HBV proteins are found in meat, fish, dairy foods, eggs and soya (the only HBV vegetable protein), and LBV proteins are found in peas, beans, nuts, lentils and cereals.

Can you see the difference? The higher level answer is much more detailed because it goes into a greater explanation and gives numerous examples. That's why in every chapter you'll find model questions and answers, to give you a flavour of these extended writing exam-style questions. Each question has two answers, both with typical examiner feedback explaining how marks are awarded. Many students lose marks simply because they don't include enough detail, so make sure you don't fall into that trap.

My goal in writing this book is to try and help you produce top grade answers in your exam – where you can select the facts you've learned and show the examiner your detailed understanding. If there is anything you aren't sure of please ask your food teacher: they will be more than willing to help because **all** teachers want their students to get the best grade they can.

If you put the effort into your revision you're giving yourself the best chance to do well in the exams – good luck!

Jayne Hill

PRINCIPLES OF NUTRITION

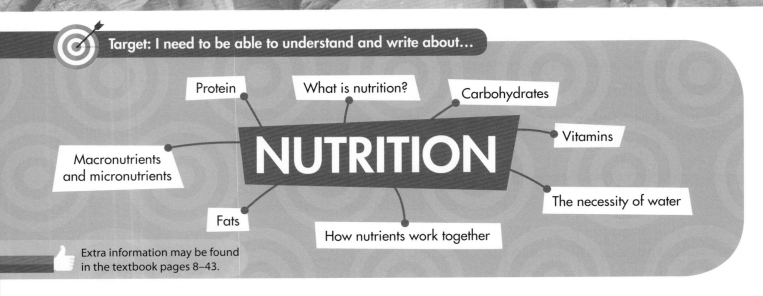

Target: I need to be able to understand and write about…

Protein

What is nutrition?

Carbohydrates

NUTRITION

Vitamins

Macronutrients and micronutrients

The necessity of water

Fats

How nutrients work together

Extra information may be found in the textbook pages 8–43.

Grade boost

Learn these key words and use them in your written work as this will show you understand the question:

Macronutrients

Micronutrients

Nutrients

Grade boost

Make sure you can give examples of macro- and micronutrients.

Do you know how many mg are in 1g?

Can you name any nutrients found in breakfast cereals? ▼

What is nutrition?

Nutrition is the study of **nutrients**, which are chemicals found in foods vital for correct bodily functioning. A lack of nutrients causes **deficiencies** and **malnourishment** in people, resulting in health problems. Nutrients are grouped into **macronutrients** and **micronutrients**.

Macronutrients

Macronutrients are proteins, carbohydrates and fats, which are needed by the body in large amounts and are measured in grams.

Micronutrients

Micronutrients are vitamins and minerals, which are needed by the body in very small amounts and are measured in mg (milligrams) or µg (micrograms).

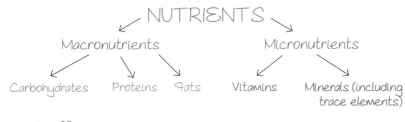

quickfire

1   Can you explain the difference between a macronutrient and a micronutrient?

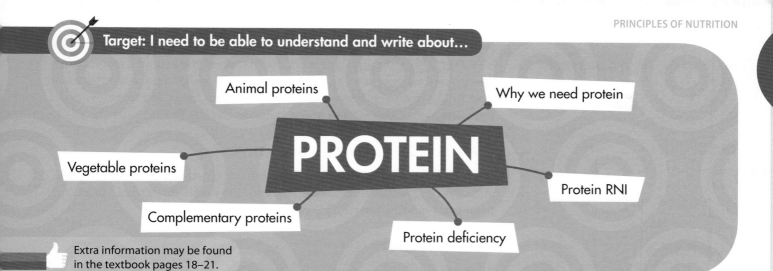

Target: I need to be able to understand and write about...

Animal proteins

Why we need protein

PROTEIN

Vegetable proteins

Protein RNI

Complementary proteins

Protein deficiency

Extra information may be found in the textbook pages 18–21.

Why we need protein

This macronutrient is vital for growth, repair, maintenance of body cells and the production of enzymes and hormones, and provides energy at 4kcal/17kJ per gram. Proteins are made from **amino acid** chains found in animal and vegetable sources.

Animal and vegetable proteins

Animal proteins have high biological values (HBVs) and are found in milk, cheese, eggs, meat and fish.

Vegetable proteins have low biological values (LBVs) and are found in seeds, nuts, beans, lentils and grains. The exceptions are soya, tofu and Quorn, which are HBV proteins.

Grade boost

Learn these key words and use them in your written work as this will show you understand the question:

Amino acid

Kwashiorkor

Oedema

Reference nutrient intake (RNI)

Grade boost

Can you state how much energy protein provides per gram?

How does this compare to the energy from 1g carbohydrate or 1g fat?

ANIMAL HBV

Lean meat, poultry and fish

Eggs

Dairy produce such as yoghurt and cheese

VEGETABLE LBV

Seeds and nuts

Beans and legumes

Grains

quickpire

2   Name five HBV proteins and five LBV proteins.

quickpire

3   How many essential amino acids do children need?
4   Learn the name of two essential amino acids.

quickpire

5   Which other LBV proteins can be served together to form HBV meals?

What is this child probably suffering from? ▼

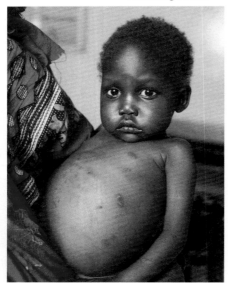

HBV and LBV refer to the number of essential amino acids in foods. HBV animal proteins and soya products contain all the essential amino acids needed in the body. LBV vegetable proteins lack one or more essential amino acid. Adults need eight essential amino acids from foods and children need the same eight plus a further seven amino acids from foods.

Complementary proteins

Putting two or more LBV proteins together will create dishes that have good amounts of essential amino acids, forming HBV meals, for example beans on toast and hummus with pitta bread.

Protein RNI

Protein **reference nutrient intake (RNI)** varies according to age and gender. On average, a person aged between 15 and 50 needs about 55g each day and a child aged 4–6 needs 20g daily.

Protein deficiency

Deficiencies are rare in the developed world – in fact we eat too much protein, which contributes to obesity and heart disease. In a famine or starvation situation children, in particular, will develop **kwashiorkor** illustrated by a failure to grow, brittle hair and 'pot' bellies due to **oedema**.

quickpire

6   How much energy is provided by 1 gram of protein?
7   Explain what HBV and LBV proteins are.
8   How can vegans make sure their diets include all the essential amino acids?

Target: I need to be able to understand and write about...

CARBOHYDRATES

Types of carbohydrate

Carbohydrate RNI

Dietary fibre/NSP

 Extra information may be found in the textbook pages 12–15.

Grade boost

Learn these key words and use them in your written work as this will show you understand the question:

Glucose

Insoluble fibre

Insulin

Soluble fibre

Starch

Sugar

These macronutrients are our main source of energy at 3.75kcal/16kJ per gram.

During digestion carbohydrates are broken down into **glucose**, which is then absorbed into the blood. The pancreas produces **insulin**, allowing glucose to enter body cells to produce energy. Some carbohydrates help rid the body of waste material (in the form of faeces).

Types of carbohydrate

Starch (complex carbohydrate) gives slow release energy, keeping us feeling fuller for longer.

Sugar (simple sugars) releases glucose very fast, giving us a short burst of energy.

Lots of factory-made foods are high in 'hidden' sugars.

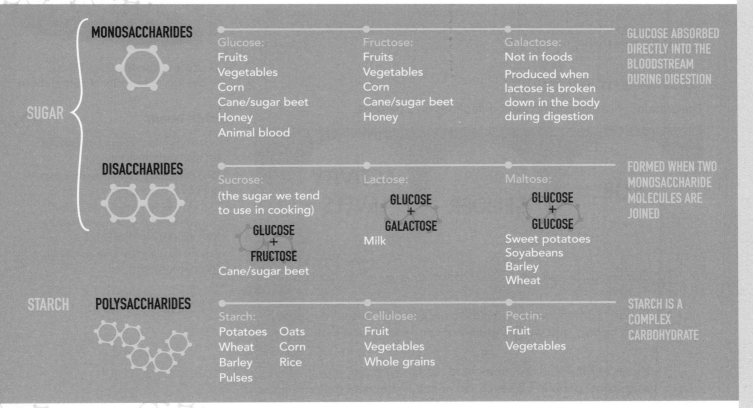

SUGAR	**MONOSACCHARIDES**	Glucose: Fruits Vegetables Corn Cane/sugar beet Honey Animal blood	Fructose: Fruits Vegetables Corn Cane/sugar beet Honey	Galactose: Not in foods Produced when lactose is broken down in the body during digestion	GLUCOSE ABSORBED DIRECTLY INTO THE BLOODSTREAM DURING DIGESTION
	DISACCHARIDES	Sucrose: (the sugar we tend to use in cooking) GLUCOSE + FRUCTOSE Cane/sugar beet	Lactose: GLUCOSE + GALACTOSE Milk	Maltose: GLUCOSE + GLUCOSE Sweet potatoes Soyabeans Barley Wheat	FORMED WHEN TWO MONOSACCHARIDE MOLECULES ARE JOINED
STARCH	**POLYSACCHARIDES**	Starch: Potatoes Oats Wheat Corn Barley Rice Pulses	Cellulose: Fruit Vegetables Whole grains	Pectin: Fruit Vegetables	STARCH IS A COMPLEX CARBOHYDRATE

QUICKFIRE

9   Name the three different types of carbohydrate sugar and give examples of each.

10   Explain what 'hidden' sugar means.

Dietary fibre/NSP

The non-starch polysaccharide (NSP) type of carbohydrate comes from all plant cells, skins and seeds.

Insoluble fibre, found in wholegrains, nuts, and many fruit and vegetables, travels through the digestive system without being digested. It is needed to absorb water and bulk out the faeces (poo), making it softer and easier to pass. It keeps the colon and bowel healthy, preventing piles, diverticulosis, diverticulitis and some cancers.

Soluble fibre, found in oats, peas, beans, carrots and apples, is digested, helping lower blood cholesterol.

A diet high in fibre keeps us feeling fuller for longer, which should stop people from snacking and help to maintain a healthy weight. Fibre also helps control our blood sugar levels, which is very important for diabetics.

quickfire

11 Plan a school packed lunch that is high in fibre.
12 Find out which three fruits and which three vegetables contain the most fibre per 100g.
13 Compare the fibre content per 100g of white bread, granary bread and wholemeal bread.

WHAT ARE DIVERTICULOSIS and DIVERTICULITIS?

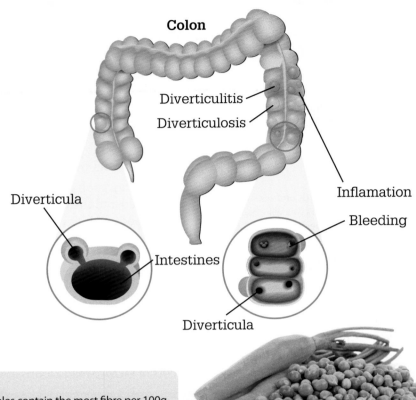

Colon

Diverticulitis

Diverticulosis

Diverticula

Intestines

Inflamation

Bleeding

Diverticula

 Sources of soluble fibre. Do you know the health benefits of eating these?

Carbohydrate RNI

The amount of carbohydrate needed depends on a person's:

AGE   GENDER   ACTIVITY LEVELS

Starchy carbohydrates should make up $\frac{1}{3}$ of all our food.

Sugary carbohydrates should be reduced because they cause tooth decay, and weight gain that can lead to type 2 diabetes.

Dietary fibre/NSP requirement for someone aged 16+ is 30g. Most people, however, do not consume enough, causing constipation, which can eventually lead to bowel diseases.

In general, eating too many carbohydrates may lead to weight gain, type 2 diabetes and heart disease.

Grade boost

Learn how much energy is provided by 1g of carbohydrate.

Why does sugar carbohydrate affect our blood sugar levels so much?

Can you explain why tooth decay is caused more by sugar carbohydrate than starchy carbohydrate?

Explain the vital role that dietary fibre/NSP has in the diet.

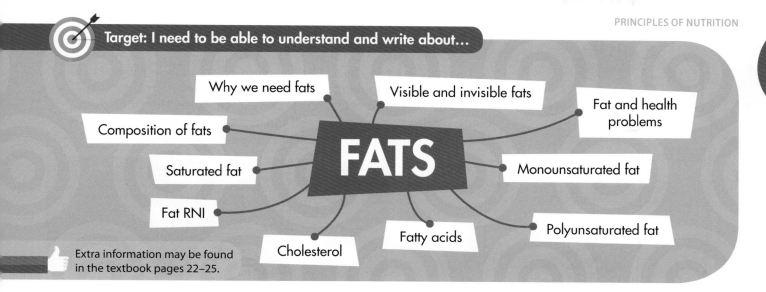

Target: I need to be able to understand and write about…

- Why we need fats
- Visible and invisible fats
- Fat and health problems
- Composition of fats
- **FATS**
- Monounsaturated fat
- Saturated fat
- Fat RNI
- Cholesterol
- Fatty acids
- Polyunsaturated fat

Extra information may be found in the textbook pages 22–25.

Why we need fats

Fat is a macronutrient which provides energy at 9kcal (37kJ) per gram. Fat is also needed for:

 WARMTH Insulation and body warmth

 PROTECT Protecting the vital organs (e.g. heart, liver, kidneys and lungs)

 TRANSIT Acting as a carrier for the fat soluble vitamins: Vitamin A, D, E and K

 HORMONES Hormone production

 FATS Supplying essential fatty acids, which the body is unable to make for itself

Grade boost

Learn these key words and use them in your written work as this will show you understand the question:

Low density lipoprotein (LDL) cholesterol

Monounsaturated fat

Polyunsaturated fat

Saturated fat

Unsaturated fats

Butter – great content but don't overdo it! ▼

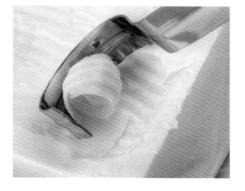

Lard: a meat fat high in LDL cholesterol levels – not good! ▼

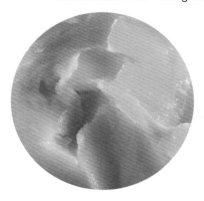

Composition of fats

All fat molecules contain carbon, hydrogen and oxygen, but how the molecules are arranged will determine the type of fat it is.

Saturated fat

Saturated fats have all the carbon atoms in each molecule joined (saturated) with hydrogen atoms. These are found mainly in animal fats and are linked with raised **low density lipoprotein (LDL) cholesterol** levels associated with coronary heart disease. Examples are butter, ghee, cream, cheese and meat fat.

Monounsaturated fat

Monounsaturated fat has one carbon atom in each molecule joined to one other carbon atom, forming a double bond. The double bond blocks any hydrogen molecule from joining the two carbon atoms. This fat helps to reduce LDL (bad) blood cholesterol and increase **high density lipoprotein (HDL) (good) cholesterol**. Examples include avocados and olive oil.

▲ Why are avocados and olive oil good fat sources?

Polyunsaturated fat

Polyunsaturated fat is where several carbon atoms form double bonds thus reducing the hydrogen atoms available in the molecule. This provides HDL cholesterol and is a good source of omega 3 and omega 6 fatty acids. Examples are sunflower, soya beans and oily fish.

quickfire

14 Give two fat sources for each type of fat.
15 Explain what a double bond is.

Grade boost

Make sure you know *why* we need fat.
Can you state the difference in look between saturated and unsaturated fat?

quickfire

16 What do you understand by the terms LDL and HDL?

Can you see how the fat has built up inside the artery? It has caused a blockage preventing blood from easily flowing through. ▼

Fatty acids

Essential fatty acids are vital for good health and are found in eggs, meat, oily fish and vegetable oils.

Cholesterol

Cholesterol is a fatty substance that is naturally occurring in the blood. It is made in the body and obtained from fatty foods. Raised cholesterol levels in the blood stream can cause arteries to block.

LDL cholesterol is unhealthy and the intake of it should be reduced.

HDL cholesterol is a healthier type of fat that helps to reduce the risk of heart attacks and strokes.

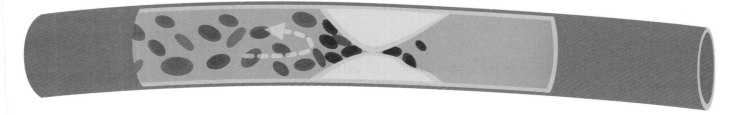

Visible and invisible fats

Visible fats can be seen, such as butter, margarine and the white fat on meat.

Invisible fats can't be seen in products such as milk, cream, nuts, avocados and many ready-made meals.

quickfire

17 Name three meat cuts containing visible fats.
18 Name three manufactured foods containing invisible fats.

Fat RNI

All diets must contain fats – and the RNI is 70g for women and 95g for men. A fat deficiency means a lack of vitamins A, D, E and K, which can lead to night-blindness, dry, brittle nails and hair, and depression. The Western diet makes it very difficult to become deficient in fat.

Fat and health problems

Eating too many fats and fatty foods causes a range of health problems, including weight gain, obesity, type 2 diabetes, blocked arteries leading to coronary heart disease, stroke and some cancers. Accepted advice is to reduce our total fat intake and eat mainly **unsaturated fats**.

Grade boost

Learn how much energy is provided by 1g of fat.

Can you explain the differences between saturated and unsaturated fats?

Do you understand the difference between HDL and LDL fats?

Describe the process of how fat can block arteries. How will this affect a person?

▲ Are you able to explain how atherosclerosis can build up in an artery?

quickfire

19 How could you make a traditional fried breakfast healthier?

Water soluble vitamins

VITAMINS

Fat soluble vitamins

Why we need vitamins

Extra information may be found in the textbook pages 26–32.

Grade boost

Learn these key words and use them in your written work as this will show you understand the question:

Anaemia

Collagen

Deficiency

Fortified

Osteomalacia

Vegan

Why we need vitamins

These micronutrients are essential in very small quantities. They are measured in units of milligrams (mg) or even smaller micrograms (μg). The body needs a wide range of vitamins to function properly and for good health. Each vitamin has specific jobs but in general they help the body to:

- release energy
- prevent some diseases
- assist in cell function and repair.

Fat soluble vitamins

Vitamins A, D, E and K are found in fats and foods naturally containing fats and oils. These vitamins can be stored in the liver and fat reserves for later use. Eating too much of these causes the body harm.

VITAMIN A

Retinol

WHY IS IT NEEDED?	WHERE IS IT FOUND?	NOT ENOUGH OF IT?	TOO MUCH OF IT?
• Healthy immune system • Helps us to see in dim light	• Liver, dairy foods, egg yolk, oily fish, yellow fruits, yellow, red and green veg	• A **deficiency** is rare but can cause night blindness, stunted growth of children	• Fractures in old age • Pregnant women eating too much can cause birth defects

VITAMIN D

Cholecalciferol the 'sunshine' vitamin

WHY IS IT NEEDED?	WHERE IS IT FOUND?	NOT ENOUGH OF IT?	TOO MUCH OF IT?
• Formation of bones and teeth • Controls calcium absorption	• Oily fish, eggs, liver, sunlight onto the skin	• Deficiency causes rickets in children or **osteomalacia** in adults • Heart failure	• Kidney damage

VITAMIN E

Tocopherol

WHY IS IT NEEDED?	WHERE IS IT FOUND?	NOT ENOUGH OF IT?	TOO MUCH OF IT?
• Anti-oxidant to prevent body from getting diseases • Healthy skin and eyes	• Soya, olive oil, nuts, seeds, milk, egg yolk	• Deficiency is unlikely	• Affects blood coagulation

VITAMIN K

WHY IS IT NEEDED?	WHERE IS IT FOUND?	NOT ENOUGH OF IT?	TOO MUCH OF IT?
• Blood clotting, wound healing • Good bone health	• Green, leafy veg, liver and bacon, cereals, vegetable oils	• Deficiency is unlikely	• Stored in the liver

Water soluble vitamins

- The B group of vitamins and vitamin C cannot be stored in the body so must be eaten every day. Any excess of these vitamins is flushed out in our urine.
- They are easily destroyed by heat, water and exposure to air during storage, preparation and cooking.
- So, don't prepare them until you need them and cook them in the smallest amount of water possible for the shortest amount of time.
- Steaming rather than boiling vegetables will preserve water soluble vitamins, and any cooking liquid could be used in sauces and gravy.
- The best way to get these vitamins is to eat fruit and vegetables raw.

B GROUP VITAMINS	WHY IS IT NEEDED?	WHERE IS IT FOUND?	NOT ENOUGH OF IT?	TOO MUCH OF IT?	
	• Releasing energy from food • Nervous system • Growth in children	• Cereal, wholegrains, eggs, dairy foods, Marmite, green leafy veg, red meat, liver	• Muscle wasting, dry, sore skin, some **anaemias**	• Unlikely because it is flushed out in urine	

VITAMIN C Ascorbic acid	WHY IS IT NEEDED?	WHERE IS IT FOUND?	NOT ENOUGH OF IT?	TOO MUCH OF IT?	
	• **Collagen** formation • Wound healing • Helps absorption of iron	• Citrus fruits, berries, tomatoes, peppers, dark green, leafy veg	• Bleeding gums, wounds not healing • Anaemia if not enough iron is absorbed	• An excess is flushed out in urine	

It is easy for vegans to be deficient in vitamin B12 because it is found mainly in liver, red meat and dairy products. It is in yeast and **fortified** cereals but in low levels. **Vegans** need to be aware of this.

quickfire

20 Which two fruits and two vegetables contain the most vitamin C per 100g?

What vitamins are found in these colourful fruit and vegetables? ▶

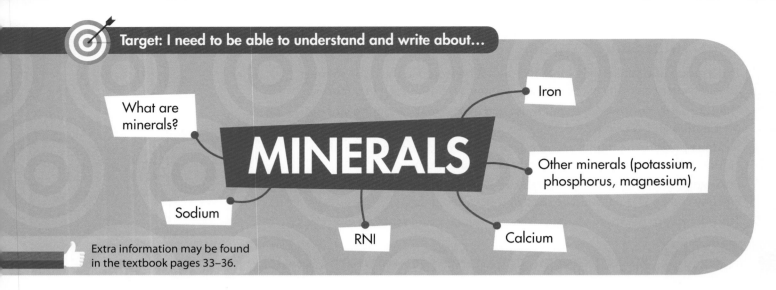

MINERALS

- What are minerals?
- Iron
- Other minerals (potassium, phosphorus, magnesium)
- Sodium
- RNI
- Calcium

Extra information may be found in the textbook pages 33–36.

Grade boost

Learn these key words and use them in your written work as this will show you understand the question:

Osteoporosis

Rickets

What are minerals?

Minerals are micronutrients essential to the body in very small quantities and are measured in units of mg (milligrams) and µg (micrograms). They are found in most foods.

The three minerals you really need to know and understand are:

- **calcium**
- **iron**
- **sodium.**

Mineral	Why is it needed?	Where is it found?	Not enough of it?	Too much of it?
Calcium	Form, strengthen and maintain bones and teeth Blood clotting For muscles and nerves of the heart	Milk, dairy food, dark green, leafy veg, wholegrain cereals, fortified soya milk	**Rickets** in children Osteomalacia in adults **Osteoporosis**	A build-up in the kidneys can be fatal
Iron	To make blood haemoglobin, which carries oxygen to cells	Red meat, liver, wholegrain cereals, beans, nuts, dark green, leafy veg	Anaemia – tired, lethargic and very pale eye margins	Constipation and nausea
Sodium	Maintains water levels in all cells Controls nerves and muscles	Salt, and 'hidden' in processed foods, bacon, burgers, tomatoes, stock cubes	Rare	High blood pressure and strokes

Other minerals

Potassium is needed for healthy blood pressure, to balance body fluids and to prevent cramps. Found in fruit, vegetables, beans, nuts and seeds.

Phosphorous works with calcium to form strong bones and teeth. Found in red meat, dairy foods and bread.

Magnesium helps bone development and the nervous system. Found in meat, fish and dairy foods.

RNI

The RNI of each mineral depends on a person's gender, age and general health. A deficiency always causes serious problems. Sodium (salt) causes a major health issue in the UK because people regularly eat more than the recommended 6g of salt a day, resulting high blood pressure and leading to strokes.

quickfire

21 What is the difference between rickets and osteomalacia?

22 What foods will provide a vegetarian with calcium and iron?

23 Name three foods that contain 'hidden' salt.

quickfire

24 The daily RNI of sodium is 2.4g but salt is 6g. Explain why are these figures so different?

Target: I need to be able to understand and write about...

Trace elements

NUTRIENTS THAT WORK TOGETHER AND WATER

How nutrients work together

Water

Extra information may be found in the textbook pages 36–38.

How nutrients work together

Some nutrients rely on each other to improve absorption.

Vitamin C + Iron: when you eat iron-rich plant sources add a vitamin C food to the dish to increase the iron absorption, for example blueberries with breakfast cereal or tomatoes in a bean salad.

Vitamin D + Calcium: you may eat lots of calcium-rich foods but if vitamin D is missing the calcium can't be absorbed and you may suffer with **calcium deficiency**. To improve this, eat a yoghurt sitting outside in the sun or a tuna sandwich with a glass of milk.

quickfire

25 Can you think of other dishes that include vitamin D + calcium or vitamin C + iron?

Trace elements

A healthy, balanced diet ensures that iodine, zinc, fluoride and selenium trace elements are easily accessed.

quickfire

26 Why is each trace element needed and where is it found?

Water

Water is not a nutrient but it is essential for life because it:

| regulates body temperature | transports nutrients in the blood | removes waste from cells | aids digestion |

We obtain water from all drinks and foods we eat. A lack of water causes **dehydration** resulting in headaches, thirst, dizziness and poor concentration.

Do you know how much water the body needs each day? If not, read on! ▶

Grade boost

Learn these key words and use them in your written work as this will show you understand the question:

Calcium deficiency

Dehydration

▲ What vitamins does this meal provide?

Grade boost

Make sure you can write a few sentences about calcium, iron and sodium.

Which vitamin works with iron?

Which vitamin works with calcium?

EXAM QUESTIONS

1   State two functions of protein.

[i] _____

_____

[ii] _____

_____

2   Explain what HBV means.

_____

_____

3   State two foods that are good sources of vegetable protein.

[i] _____

[ii] _____

4   Give three reasons why fat is necessary in the diet.

[i] _____

[ii] _____

[iii] _____

5   Describe the consequences of a high fat diet.

_____

_____

_____

_____

6   What is meant by the term 'hidden' fat?

_____

_____

_____

_____

7   Discuss the choice and uses of fats in food preparation and cooking.

_____

_____

_____

_____

8   Explain why dietary fibre is important in the diet.

_____

_____

_____

_____

9   Identify two fat soluble vitamins and two water soluble vitamins.

_____

_____

_____

_____

10   Discuss the health problems caused by a vitamin C deficiency.

_____

_____

_____

_____

11   Why might a vegan become deficient in vitamin B12?

_____

_____

_____

_____

12   Discuss three ways an adult could reduce their salt intake.

[i] _____

[ii] _____

[iii] _____

13   Explain why vitamin C and iron should be eaten in the same meal.

_____

_____

_____

_____

Sample exam question and answers with commentaries

Q1 Discuss the importance of carbohydrates in the diet.

Model answer

Carbohydrates are found in all plant foods. They are a good source of energy, supplying 3.75kcals per 1 gram and we should eat 1/3 of our daily calorie intake from starchy carbohydrates.

They are either starchy or sugar. The sugar carbs are monosaccharides such as fruits, vegetables, sugar and honey or disaccharides such as sugar, milk and wheat. Sugars are in most processed foods and are classed as 'hidden' sugars. These can cause dental decay, obesity and type 2 diabetes. So we should eat this type of carbohydrate sparingly.

Starchy carbs are polysaccharides-complex carbs and are found in cereals, pulses, vegetables and rice. We should consume more starch than sugary carbs because they keep us fuller for longer. This should stop us from snacking on sugary and fatty foods.

Dietary fibre or NSP is what the cell walls, pips, skins and seeds of fruit, vegetables, pulses and grains are called. We should eat 30g of fibre a day to prevent constipation, bowel diseases such as diverticulosis and some cancers.

Commentary

An excellent, detailed answer that would get the top band of marks. The student has both knowledge and understanding of carbohydrates. Recall of carbohydrate facts – energy, sources, types – is good and these facts are linked in to the diet and health issue, which shows a good understanding.

Weaker answer

Carbohydrates give us energy. If we eat too many of them we will get fat and have bad teeth. Bread, potatoes, pastry, jam and sugar are carbs. Overweight people get heart disease and diabetes 2 so it can shorten your life. Some carbohydrates help us to poo easier and they can help us stay full up for longer.

Commentary

This answer shows some factual knowledge linked to health issues. There is no reference to starch, sugar and fibre/NSP. Compare the information given here to the information in the model answer. The marks awarded would be low down in the middle band.

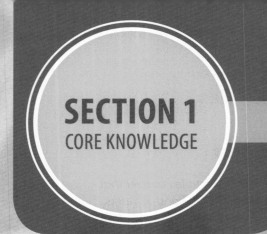

Target: I need to be able to understand and write about...

What a 'healthy' diet is

Healthy eating guidelines

Special dietary needs

DIET AND GOOD HEALTH

Individual nutritional needs

Vegetarianism

Religious beliefs

Extra information may be found in the textbook pages 45–67.

Grade boost

Learn these key words and use them in your written work as this will show you understand the question:

Allergy

Eatwell Guide

Eight top tips

Intolerances

Lacto vegetarians

Lacto-ovo vegetarians

Vegans

quickfire

1 State the percentage of our food intake from:
   a) fruit and veg
   b) carbohydrates
   c) fats and oils.
2 Why don't potatoes count towards our 'five-a-day'?

Healthy diets

A diet refers to the foods you eat. To have a healthy diet it must contain a good **balance** of all the necessary nutrients. If too much of one nutrient is eaten then the diet becomes unbalanced and possibly unhealthy, for example snacking on sweets and crisps might mean that you aren't eating enough vegetables. To understand how to eat a healthy diet we need to understand the healthy eating guidelines.

Healthy eating guidelines

Research suggests that following the Eatwell Guide, the eight top tips for healthy eating, and including at least five fruits and vegetables in our diets, will help us to eat healthily.

Increase our intake of fibre/NSP foods, vegetables and oily fish. **REMEMBER THIS**

Reduce our intake of fat, sugar and salt. **REMEMBER THIS**

Fruit and vegetables

Bread, rice, potatoes, pasta and other starchy foods

Food and drinks high in fat and/or sugar

Oil and spreads

Milk and dairy foods

Meat, fish, eggs, beans and other non-dairy sources of protein

The Eatwell Guide recommends that our foods come mainly from the starchy carbohydrate and fruit/vegetables sections and that we should eat smaller amounts of protein and dairy foods. We should reduce the amounts of fats/oils eaten and only occasionally eat sugary foods. It is advised we have six–eight drinks per day. Following both the Eatwell Guide and the 'eight top tips' may help to prevent dietary related diseases.

Individual nutritional needs

Our nutritional needs change according to our **age**, **gender**, **activity levels** and **overall health**. For example, a teenage boy's dietary needs are different from an adult male builder; a middle-aged woman's dietary needs are different from a pregnant woman's; and a 'couch potato' has different dietary needs from Olympians.

Special dietary needs

Special dietary needs have to be considered when planning a menu, as the table below shows.

quickfire

3 What happens if energy input and energy output are not the same?

4 Name a food unit of energy.

5 State two health effects of an excessive intake of energy.

6 Name two dietary related diseases.

Grade boost

Make sure you understand and can explain the meaning of 'a balanced diet'.

Can you state the Eatwell Guide percentage of fruit and vegetables and starchy foods?

Can you state the difference between an allergy and an intolerance?

SECTION 1

SPECIAL DIETARY NEEDS

COELIAC DISEASE 	The body cannot absorb protein found in wheat, rye, barley and some oats. Bread, biscuits, cakes and sauces cannot be eaten without causing abdominal pain.
ANAEMIA 	The body lacks iron, which is needed for red blood cell production. Red meat and green, leafy vegetables will help increase iron levels.
DIABETES TYPE 2 	The body has become insulin resistant and cannot utilise the glucose produced by carbohydrates; this can result in amputations of limbs and blindness. To help prevent type 2 diabetes follow the healthy eating guidelines, exercise and control your weight.
CARDIOVASCULAR DISEASE 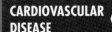	The body develops raised blood pressure, high cholesterol and blocked arteries leading to heart disease. To help prevent this take more exercise, stop smoking, control your weight and follow the healthy eating guidelines.
OBESITY 	The body takes in more energy than is used. The spare energy is stored under the skin and around the organs in a fatty layer. To prevent this exercise regularly, eat lots of vegetables, fruit and complex carbohydrates and **drastically** reduce fatty and sugary foods.
BONE AND DENTAL HEALTH 	A diet should contain foods rich in calcium **and** vitamin D. Regular exercise also helps bones to become stronger. Teeth – a good cleaning regime is needed and sweet foods and fizzy drinks should only be consumed on rare occasions.
FOOD ALLERGIES AND INTOLERANCES 	A food allergy can be serious – it might cause death, for example peanuts and shellfish. Intolerances, such as lactose and gluten, are not life threatening but will cause unpleasant symptoms.

Vegetarianism

- **Lacto-ovo vegetarians** eat dairy foods and eggs but **not** meat or fish.
- **Lacto vegetarians** eat dairy foods but **not** eggs, milk or fish.
- **Vegans** do **not** eat any animal produce (including honey).

The reasons for being vegetarian include:

Not liking animals being killed for food

Unhappy with animal welfare/factory farming

Religious beliefs

Perceived to be healthier

Cheaper

Disliking the texture or flavour of meat

Environmental concerns

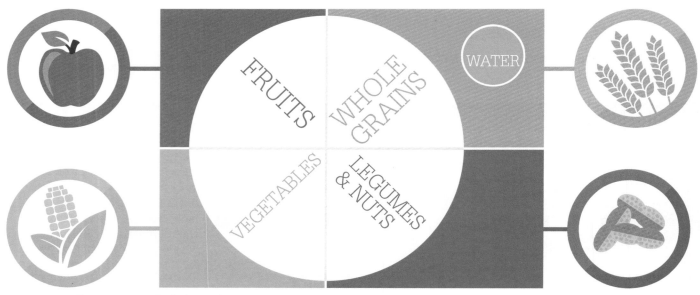

▲ Components of a balanced vegetarian or vegan diet

People need to be aware that by eliminating meat and fish from their diet is an easy way to become deficient in micronutrients such as iron and vitamin B12, and a heavy reliance on dairy foods can create a diet imbalance due to over-eating cheese and cheese products that are high in fat.

Vegans must eat a wide range of vegetable proteins to ensure they are getting all the essential amino acids. Vegans who eat only a limited range of foods can soon become nutritionally deficient, leading to serious health issues.

quickfire

7 State a non-animal source of HBV protein.

8 How do vegans get their iron intake?

What important foods are missing here that vegetarians should eat? ▼

Religious beliefs

- Many **Buddhists** are vegan or vegetarian, believing that they should not be responsible for the death of any living organism.
- **Hindus** do not eat meat from a cow, which is a sacred animal.
- Some denominations of **Christianity** say that only fish should be eaten on Fridays.
- **Jewish** food should be kosher (meat from animals that have split hoofs and that chew the cud) and slaughtered according to strict laws.
- **Muslim** food must be halal, i.e. animals killed according to Muslim law.
- **Rastafarians** eat only ital foods (natural and pure).
- **Seventh Day Adventists** are prohibited from eating animal flesh.
- **Sikhs** do not eat beef or pork.

▲ Can you name a religion that considers the cow sacred?

	BEEF	PORK	POULTRY & GOAT	FISH/ SHELLFISH	EGGS	MILK	ALCOHOL
BUDDISM	✗	✗	✗	some	✓	✓	
HINDUISM	✗	✗	Restricted/Avoided		✗		✗
JUDAISM	Kosher	✗	Kosher	✗	Kosher	Not with meat	
ISLAM	Halal	✗	Halal	✗			✗
RASTAFARIANISM	✗	✗	✗	No fish over 3cm			✗
SEVENTH DAY ADVENTIST	✗	✗	✗	✗	✓		✗
SIKH	In some sects halal or kosher						✗

▲ Summary of religious-based diets

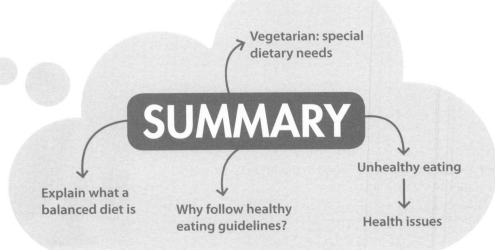

SUMMARY

- Vegetarian: special dietary needs
- Explain what a balanced diet is
- Why follow healthy eating guidelines?
- Unhealthy eating
- Health issues

EXAM QUESTIONS

1 Explain two healthy eating guidelines.

   [i] _____

   _____

   [i] _____

   _____

2 What is meant by 'energy dense'?

   _____

3 Why should you not skip breakfast?

   _____

   _____

4 How should a person with type 2 diabetes adapt their diet?

   _____

   _____

5 How could you reduce the fat used when preparing and cooking meals?

   _____

   _____

6 Discuss how to ensure a vegetarian diet is balanced.

   _____

   _____

   _____

   _____

   _____

   _____

   _____

   _____

7 Name the nutrients found in the breakfast in the photo on the right.

   _____

   _____

Sample exam questions and answers with commentaries

Q1 How could a school canteen encourage the pupils to eat more fruit and vegetables?

Model answer

The canteen could reduce the price of pieces of fruit to encourage more students to buy and eat fruit rather than expensive chocolate and cakes. They could provide raw vegetable sticks served with hummus or dips. The canteen could work with Student Voice to add vegetable-rich dishes to the menu — dishes that students would actually buy. They could have tasting sessions to encourage students to try fruit and vegetables they may never have tasted before. Students could have reward cards that are stamped every time they buy a fruit or vegetable dish which, after 20 dishes, would earn them a reward. The canteen could put colourful flyers/posters around the school.

Commentary

 This is a good answer showing clearly that the student has considered a range of ways in which the canteen could promote the uptake of fruit and vegetables.

Weak answer

Make the fruit cheaper so pupils can afford to buy it. Have a competition to see who can eat the most fruit each week. Put up adverts round the school to get pupils to buy fruit and vegetables.

Commentary

 This would receive medium band marks. The student has given three ways of promoting fruit and vegetables, however the answer lacks the detail of the model answer.

Q2 Describe the factors that influence a person's energy requirement.

Model answer

Age, gender, occupation, state of health and exercise all influence how much energy is required.

Different ages of life have different energy requirements — babies and toddlers need less than active teenagers. Men generally require more energy than females simply because they have larger bodies and more muscle mass. A person's job will influence energy intake. A sedentary office worker will need less energy intake than a builder or athlete. People who are ill need more energy to help repair their body and fight infections. However, if the person is immobile then they may need less energy intake.

Commentary

 Highest band marks would be awarded for this answer because it gives a wide range of factors influencing energy requirements. The points made have been justified, showing both knowledge and understanding of the subject.

Weak answer

People need different amounts of energy depending on their job. Men need more energy than women. If you have too much energy you will get fat.

Commentary

 Three good points made but each point needs justifying by posing the question 'why?', such as:

Why *does a person's job influence their energy requirement?*

If each point had been explained higher marks would be awarded.

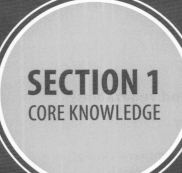

 Target: I need to be able to understand and write about…

How to prevent nutrient loss when preparing and cooking food

Why do we cook food?

The why and how of raising agents

THE SCIENCE OF COOKING FOOD

Methods of transferring heat to food

The science behind prepared and cooked foods – proteins, fats, carbohydrates, effects of oxygen, pH, enzymes, microorganisms

👍 Extra information may be found in the textbook pages 68–83.

Grade boost

Learn these key words and use them in your written work as this will show you understand the question:

Aeration	Maillard reaction
Caramelise	Microorganisms
Coagulate	Myoglobin
Conduction	Oxidising of enzymes
Convection	
Denature	Pathogenic bacteria
Dextrins	pH value
Emulsion	Plasticity
Enzymes	Radiation
Gelatinise	Rancid
Gluten	Strong flour
Heat transference	

Why do we cook food?

- To make food safe to eat – heat kills **pathogenic bacteria**.
- To soften the food, making it easier to chew, swallow and digest.
- To make it look appetising and improve the flavour.
- To warm us up – hot food in cold weather.

quicKfire

1   Give two examples of why we cook food.

When cooking food you need to choose the appropriate method.

Tough stewing steak needs long, slow, moist cooking but this cooking method would ruin tender cuts such as fillets of steak or plaice.

Methods of transferring heat to food

Food is cooked using heat, which is transferred using **conduction**, **convection** and/or **radiation** (infra-red radiant heat or microwave) through dry heat, moist heat, radiant heat or microwave energy. The type of foods cooked determines which method of **heat transference** is needed and whether the food should be cooked using a dry or moist method.

QUICKFIRE

2   State the three methods of heat transfer.
3   Write one sentence for each of the following to describe it:
    a) conduction b) convection c) radiation.
4   Name three dry methods of cooking and three moist methods of cooking.

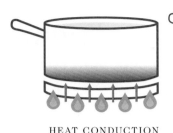

HEAT CONDUCTION IN A PAN

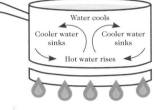

HEAT PROCESS SHOWING CONVECTION

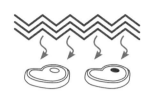

RADIANT HEAT FROM GRILL

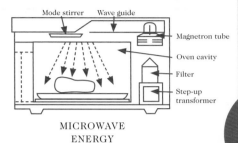

MICROWAVE ENERGY

Science behind prepared and cooked food

The size/density and appearance of all protein, fat and carbohydrate foods are affected when beaten, heated or the **pH value** is changed. The changes are permanent and cannot be undone.

Grade boost

Describe the differences between conduction, convection and radiant heat transfers.
Can you give three examples of food coagulation?

Protein

Proteins **denature** and **coagulate** when:

they are heated

QUICKFIRE

5   In no more than 140 characters describe, with examples, denaturing.
6   In no more than 140 characters describe, with examples, coagulation.
7   What changes occur when baking a shortbread biscuit?

they come into contact with acidic/alkaline ingredients

they are whisked, beaten or kneaded (foams and gluten development)

the proteins unravel becoming firm when heated.

Dry heat on meat protein creates a **Maillard reaction**.

▲ Can you see the Maillard reaction on the beef surface?

▲ Deep fat frying – such as with chips – cooks with conduction and convection

Fats

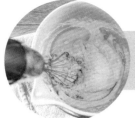

At room temperature fats can be easily spread and mixed with other ingredients. This property is called **plasticity**.

Fats melt and become liquid when heated. They add flavour and texture to cooked food, and some fat can 'melt out' from the ingredient.

quickfire

8 What is the main difference between a fat and an oil?
9 How does 'plasticity' help us when baking cakes?

Fats 'shorten' **gluten** strands in shortcrust pastry and biscuits creating a crumbly texture.

Carbohydrates

▼ Gelatinisation of starch

- **Starchy** carbohydrates, such as flour, when mixed with a liquid and heated will **gelatinise**.

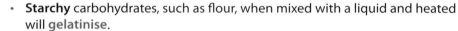

Starch granules

Starch granules softening

Starch granules swelling and absorbing water

quickfire

10 Explain and give examples for:
a) gelatinisation
b) caramelisation
c) dextrinisation.

- **Sugary** carbohydrates, such as the natural sugar in fried onions, will **caramelise** when heated.
- Starchy carbohydrates when exposed to **dry** heat create **dextrins**.

▲ What is the term for the browning of these onions?

▲ How do you know that this bread is dextrinised?

pH

Foods are either acidic, neutral or alkaline, which are all measured using the pH scale. The addition of acidic or alkaline ingredients will change the texture and appearance of some foods.

Acidic ingredients include tomatoes, vinegar, and lemon and lime juices. Bicarbonate of soda is an alkaline ingredient.

Oxygen

Oxygen can have a negative effect on many foods:

- Fruit and vegetables – cut surfaces can go brown due to **oxidising of enzymes**.
- Meat – the red surface becomes brown/grey due to oxygen affecting the **myoglobin**.
- Fish – oxygen works with fish **enzymes** making it spoil rapidly and smell very fishy.
- Fats and oils – oxygen turns fats and oils **rancid**.

▲ How has oxygen affected the meat?

▲ What makes bananas go brown once they have been peeled?

Emulsification

An **emulsion** is where oil and water join together in suspension (so they don't separate out).

To emulsify oil and water an **emulsifier** is needed such as adding egg yolk to the mixture.

Sunflower oil + Vinegar + Egg yolk = Mayonnaise

Other examples of emulsification are creamed cake mixtures, milk, butter and vegetable fat spread.

quickfire

11 Describe how the acid in lemon juice affects raw meat, egg whites and milk.

12 Why would you marinade meat in a tomato, lemon juice and yoghurt mixture?

quickfire

13 In one sentence explain what an emulsion is.

14 Which ingredients, in a creamed cake mixture, are emulsified?

SECTION 1

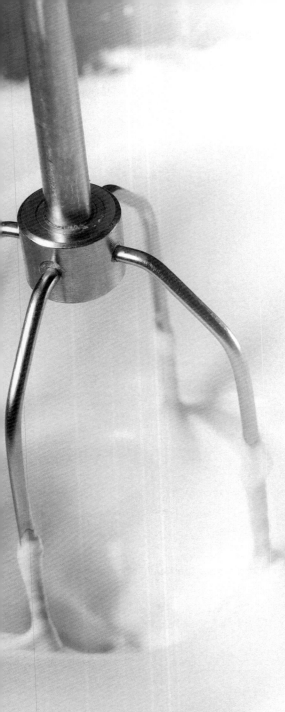

Enzymes

Enzymes are needed to soften, flavour and ripen many foods. Apples become sweet, while freshly slaughtered meat relies on enzyme activity to soften the muscle fibres.

However, enzymes will continue to work, causing food decay, with foods developing slimy textures and unpleasant flavours.

Microorganisms

Yeasts, moulds and 'safe' bacteria have been used in food production for centuries. They are used when making bread, cheese and some milk products such as yoghurt. The microorganisms affect the texture, flavour and shelf life of the foods.

QUICKFIRE

15 Name two cheeses that use bacteria in production.
16 Which microorganism is used in bread making?
17 State the microorganism that is used to produce yoghurt and lassi milk.

Raising agents

▲ Why is flour sieved?

Aeration

Aeration, the addition of air to food, will lighten the texture and/or help it rise because air particles expand on heating. Air can be added to a mixture by sieving, beating, laminating or whisking.

Steam

Steam is produced in oven-baked products, creating a puffed-up, risen effect. The original mixture must have a high volume of liquid, as in choux pastry and batter mixes.

QUICKFIRE

18 Name three dishes where steam is used to create the rise.

Chemical raising agents

Carbon dioxide is produced when self-raising flour, baking powder and bicarbonate of soda are mixed with a liquid and heated. The CO_2 gas produces bubbles, which 'push up' the food giving a light, risen texture.

QUICKFIRE

19 Name two dishes that can be made with:
   a) self-raising flour
   b) baking powder
   c) bicarbonate of soda.

Can you see the laminations in this flaky pastry? ▼

Yeast

Yeast needs food, moisture, warmth and time to grow, and will then give off lots of CO_2 bubbles, creating the light, airy, risen texture of bread. To make a successful yeasted bread strong flour must be used.

QUICKFIRE

20 Why is it important to use strong flour when bread making?

CAN YOU IDENTIFY THE DIFFERENT RAISING AGENTS AT WORK IN THESE DISHES?

SECTION 1

Can you name the missing ingredient in this photo that is necessary to make the bread dough? ▼

EXAM QUESTIONS

1   Give three reasons, with examples, of why food is cooked.

[i] _____

[ii] _____

[iii] _____

2   Describe how convection currents transfer heat to food.

_____

_____

3   Describe how conduction heat transfers to food.

_____

_____

4   State and explain one change that happens when heating starch in a sauce or gravy.

_____

_____

5   State and explain one change that happens when whisking egg white into a foam.

_____

_____

6   Name four conditions needed to activate yeast.

[i] _____   [iii] _____

[ii] _____   [iv] _____

7   Name an alternative raising agent to commercial yeast for bread making.

_____

8   Describe the changes that occur when making shortcrust pastry.

_____

_____

_____

9   State the changes that happen when boiling pasta.

_____

_____

_____

_____

Sample exam question and answers with commentaries

Q1 State the changes that occur when baking a cake.

Model answer

When a cake mixture is cooked the egg and wheat proteins denature when heated, coagulating to create a firm structure. The starch in the flour converts into dextrins forming a golden brown surface. The caster sugar caramelises adding flavour and colour to the cake. The self-raising flour (or baking powder) produces CO_2 when it becomes moist and then heated, which creates a light, airy, risen cake.

Commentary

This is a very good answer because all aspects of the cake making process have been discussed. It shows clear knowledge and understanding of how and what happens when a cake is baked.

Weaker answer

When you mix the cake ingredients together it forms a batter. When this is put into the oven it rises up and goes harder. The cake goes brown.

Commentary

This is a low mark, basic answer. The second and third statements need 'how?' and 'why?' answering.

Q2 Name two tough cuts of meat. State how tough cuts can be made tender.

Model answer

Beef: stewing/braising/chuck/skirt/flank/shin; pork: belly; lamb: shank/breast; chicken: thighs/legs.

Tough cuts of meat are found in well used muscle making the fibres very strong. They come from the abdomen, legs and shoulders of animals. Tough cuts must be cooked slowly, usually in a liquid, for a long time, e.g. beef stew or coq au vin. Certain acidic ingredients can be added to the cooking liquid to help tenderise the meat, such as tinned tomatoes, or a splash of vinegar or lemon juice. The acid in these foods helps to soften the collagen fibres in the muscle. Tough meat can also be marinaded in lemon juice or tomato-based sauces to soften the fibres.

Commentary

This response would achieve high marks because the candidate is able to name correctly tough cuts of meat.

The explanation given is clearly expressed and identifies why certain meat cuts are tough and where they are found on the animal carcass. Three ways of softening tough cuts have been identified.

Weak answer

Beef and pork for roasting.
You need to cook them for a long time, like roasting some beef.

Commentary

This answer would gain very low marks. The candidate has not stated cuts of meat; they've just named two types. This type of mistake is regularly made by candidates.

How to tenderise tough cuts has not been explained. Roasting needs justifying as it is possible to roast tender meat cuts also.

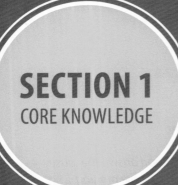

 Target: I need to be able to understand and write about...

- What causes food spoilage?
- How to store foods safely
- Preserving foods safely

FOOD SPOILAGE

- Pathogenic bacteria and food poisoning
- Cooking foods safely (key temperatures)
- HACCP

👍 Extra information may be found in the textbook pages 84–91.

Grade boost

Learn these key words and use them in your written work as this will show you understand the question:

Ambient foods	High-risk foods
Bacteria	Hot-held foods
Binary fission	Moulds
Campylobacter	Pathogenic
Chilled foods	Perishable foods
Core temperature	Preserve
Cross-contamination	Salmonella
E. coli	Staph A.
Frozen foods	Yeasts

Causes of food spoilage

CAUSES OF FOOD SPOILAGE

MICROORGANISMS

bacteria, moulds, yeasts, fungi

CHEMICAL REACTIONS

the reactions between the food, oxygen and moisture

ENVIRONMENTAL FACTORS

such as warmth, pH, oxygen and moisture

TIME

the speed of spoilage is determined by hygiene, correct storage and temperatures

INSECTS AND RODENTS

leave behind bacteria, urine and faeces

ENZYMES

speed up the process of decay to enable bacteria to absorb nutrients and reproduce

Foods spoil and decay due to microorganisms such as enzymes, **yeasts**, **moulds** and **bacteria**. If microorganism growth is controlled, most spoilage and decay can be slowed down. The Food Safety Act of 1990 informs all food producers how to keep their products safe for consumption. Food safety relies on correct storage procedures, hygienic preparation and temperature control when cooking/processing and reheating foods to prevent **pathogenic** bacterial growth.

Good hygiene is critical when storing and preparing food because dirty hands, unclean equipment, coughing and licking fingers will introduce pathogenic bacteria to food. Bacteria cannot move on their own; they need a vehicle, which is usually our hands and equipment. Moving bacteria from one place to another is called **cross-contamination**, making the food unsafe to eat.

Environmental Health Officers (EHOs) are responsible for monitoring all food businesses to check that food safety regulations are being adhered to. If the EHO finds poor practices the business owner will be warned, fined or jailed, depending on how serious the problem is.

▲ Why does the fruit look like this?

quickfire

1 What is 'pathogenic' bacteria?
2 Name three pathogenic bacteria.
3 State three ways of cross-contaminating food.

Bacteria types, sources and harm caused ▼

Pathogenic bacterium	Where it is found	Typical symptoms	Average onset time
Campylobacter	Raw poultry, meat, milk, sewage	Abdominal pain, diarrhoea (bloody), nausea, fever	48–60 hours
Salmonella	Intestines of humans and animals, raw poultry and meat, eggs, milk	Abdominal pain, diarrhoea, nausea, vomiting	12–36 hours
Staphylococcus A.	Humans – skin, hair, nose, mouth, throat, cuts, spots	Abdominal pain/cramps, vomiting, chills	1–6 hours
E. coli	Human and animal sewage, water, raw meat, muddy vegetables	Abdominal pain, fever, diarrhoea, vomiting, kidney damage/failure	12–24 hours

Storage of food

Foods must be stored in correct temperature conditions to slow down bacterial growth and food spoilage.

- **Chilled foods** – fridge at **5°C**
- **Frozen foods** – freezer at **–18°C** or colder
- **Ambient foods** – stored on a shelf or in a cupboard at **room** temperature
- **Hot-held foods** – cooked foods must be kept **63°C** or above on hot-food counters

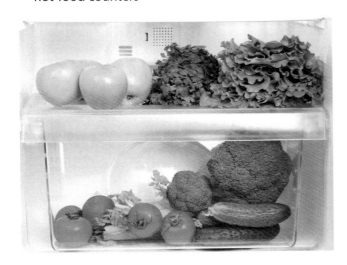

◀ Food should be stored in a fridge at 5°C. Why is this?

quickfire

4 Can you explain the following words:
a) microorganisms
b) enzymes
c) yeast
d) moulds
e) bacteria
f) pathogenic
g) cross-contamination
h) perishable
i) core temperature?

Grade boost

Learn the critical temperatures of –18°C, 5°C, 63°C and 75°C. Are you able to say why these temperatures are so important?

Do you understand how to reduce food waste and can you explain why it is an environmental problem?

How can good personal hygiene prevent food poisoning?

SECTION 1

How do you remember which cutting board to use?

- **Red** – blood is red, raw meat is bloody
- **Blue** – the sea is blue and fish come from the sea
- **Green** – lettuce is green and is a salad vegetable
- **Yellow** – ham often has yellow breadcrumbs around the edges
- **White** – dairy foods are made from white milk
- **Brown** – muddy vegetables; mud is brown

Preparing foods safely

Safe food preparation procedures will minimise the growth of pathogenic bacteria. The biggest food health risk is cross-contamination. So, food handlers must always have clean hands, and use clean equipment and different-coloured boards.

COLOUR CODED CUTTING BOARDS

eliminate the risk of bacterial cross-contamination during food preparation

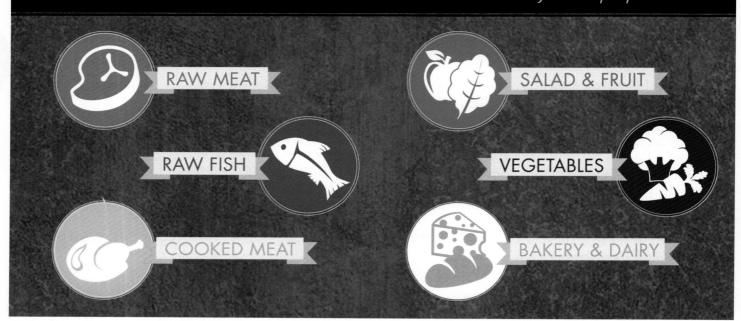

RAW MEAT

SALAD & FRUIT

RAW FISH

VEGETABLES

COOKED MEAT

BAKERY & DAIRY

Preserving foods safely

With the correct conditions bacteria will double every 10–20 minutes, which is called **binary fission**. So food needs to be **preserved** in some way to minimise bacterial growth, moulds and food spoilage. This is achieved by:

- controlling the storage temperature **or**
- removing the moisture/air **or**
- changing the pH **or**
- high cooking temperatures.

Bacteria are just like us because to grow they also need oxygen, moisture, warmth, food and time. **REMEMBER THIS**

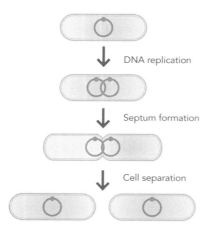

DNA replication

Septum formation

Cell separation

▲ Binary fission is how bacteria divide and multiply.

WHAT HAPPENS WHEN ...   PRESERVATION METHOD   FOOD EXAMPLES

WHAT HAPPENS WHEN ...	PRESERVATION METHOD	FOOD EXAMPLES
AIR REMOVED	Vacuum packing, cans, jars	Part-baked baguettes, ham, canned foods
MOISTURE REMOVED	Drying	Dried milk and soups, gravy granules
pH CHANGED	Pickling/jam making	Pickles, jams, salted meats
HEAT TREATED	Pasteurisation, canning	Orange juice, canned meats

Pathogenic bacteria and food poisoning

Pathogenic bacteria multiply on **high-risk foods** if the correct rules for storage, preparation, cooking and reheating are not followed.

High-risk foods are moist protein foods such as chicken, fish, prawns and cream. **REMEMBER THIS**

Food poisoning symptoms include nausea, vomiting, diarrhoea, headache and fever. **REMEMBER THIS**

Food poisoning bacteria are:
Salmonella, Campylobacter, E. coli and **Staph A.** **REMEMBER THIS**

Cooking foods safely

The core of all cooked food must be 'piping hot' or 75°C to be sure that most pathogenic bacteria are killed. Once the food has reached at **least 75°C** it should be served immediately, hot-held **above 63°C** or chilled to 5°C within **90 minutes** of cooking.

Most foods are cooked or heat-treated **before** being preserved, for example blanching vegetables before freezing or cooking fruit during the canning process.

QUICKFIRE

10   In one sentence describe each one of the following processes:
    a) pickling   b) freezing   c) canning   d) drying.

SECTION 1

QUICKFIRE

5   State five ideal conditions that bacteria need to grow.

6   Why does storing **perishable foods** in a fridge only preserve food temporarily?

7   Name two ingredients that can change the pH of foods.

QUICKFIRE

8   State three high-risk dishes.

9   Name two food-poisoning bacteria. State where they are found and what symptoms they produce.

Grade boost

Name three pathogenic bacteria.

Refer to the four critical temperatures in your written work, which are −18°C, 5°C, 63°C and 75°C.

Can you describe two methods of preserving food?

11 State two biological, chemical and physical forms of contamination.

12 Using no more than 140 characters, write a Tweet to explain how cross-contamination occurs.

HACCP

The law states that all food businesses **must** have a **H**azard **A**nalysis **C**ritical **C**ontrol **P**oint (HACCP) assessment document to keep both the food products and the customers safe. During the making/manufacture process of food products each stage must be monitored and recorded to prove that all safety regulations have been followed. A HACCP should **save** food from biological, chemical or physical contamination that could harm customers.

The HACCP for fish ▼

STAGE	HAZARD	CONTROL
Accepting delivery of fresh fish	Is the van clean and refrigerated? Is packaging undamaged? Is fish 5°C or delivered on ice?	The supplier is reputable Check temperature Packaging not damaged
Storing the fish	Not stored at correct temperature allowing bacterial growth Not needed for two days	Place in the fridge at 5°C Bottom shelf of fridge or fish fridge Wrap/cover and date fish Store in freezer
Using the fish	Removing fish from the fridge too early Unclean surfaces, hands and equipment	Remove from the fridge only when needed Clean and sanitise all surfaces, equipment and hands before and after handling the fish
Cooking fish	Incorrectly cooked	Core temperature 75°C
Serving fish	Cooked fish left on the kitchen 'side' – everyone busy	Serve immediately Do not allow the fish to fall into the danger zone – below 63°C

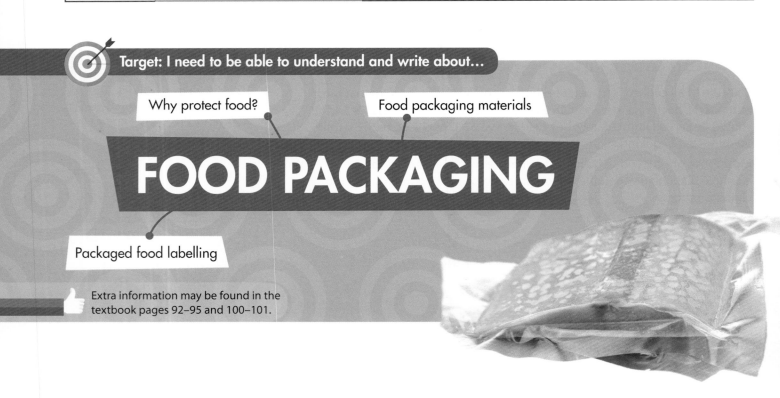

Target: I need to be able to understand and write about…

Why protect food?

Food packaging materials

FOOD PACKAGING

Packaged food labelling

👍 Extra information may be found in the textbook pages 92–95 and 100–101.

Why protect food?

Packaging is used to protect food:

- to stop cross-contamination from:
  - physical contamination
  - chemical contamination
  - biological contamination
- to keep food hygienic and safe to eat
- for ease of handling and transporting foods
- to provide important information on labels
- to stop it from getting damaged.

Food packaging materials

Paper, paperboard and cardboard are used for pizza take-aways, eggs, juice cartons.

Plastic is used in lots of packaging, such as for milk, yoghurt, cheese, sandwiches, vegetables.

Cans and foil are used for vegetables, fruit, meat, fish, ready-made dinners.

Glass is used for jam, chutneys, pickles, bottled drinks.

Modified atmosphere packaging (MAP) contains controlled amounts of O_2, CO_2 and nitrogen to slow down food spoilage. It is used to package cooked and raw meats/fish and some fresh fruit.

How modified atmosphere packaging (MAP) works in bagged salad ▼

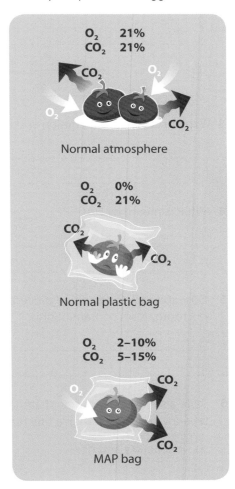

O_2 21%
CO_2 21%

Normal atmosphere

O_2 0%
CO_2 21%

Normal plastic bag

O_2 2–10%
CO_2 5–15%

MAP bag

SECTION 1

Packaged food labelling

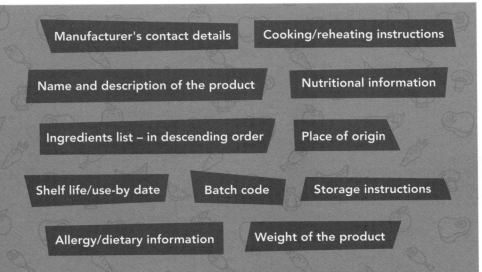

- Manufacturer's contact details
- Cooking/reheating instructions
- Name and description of the product
- Nutritional information
- Ingredients list – in descending order
- Place of origin
- Shelf life/use-by date
- Batch code
- Storage instructions
- Allergy/dietary information
- Weight of the product

Grade boost

Learn this key word and use it in your written work as this will show you understand the question:
Modified atmosphere packaging (MAP)

quickfire

13 State two advantages and two disadvantages of each packaging material.

14 Which of the packaging materials listed above CAN be recycled?

EXAM QUESTIONS

1 Name three food poisoning bacteria.

_____

_____

_____

2 What does 'binary fission' mean?

_____

_____

_____

3 Explain cross-contamination and how to prevent it.

_____

_____

4 What is meant by HACCP?

_____

_____

5 Describe how food can be prevented from microorganism contamination.

_____

_____

6 State a suitable packaging material for each of the take-away dishes **and** give one reason for your choice:

a) beef curry and rice _____

_____

_____

b) hot BLT sandwich _____

_____

_____

7 UK food outlets produce over **three million tonnes** of waste per year. Discuss how a food business can reduce its food, non-food **and** packaging waste.

_____

_____

_____

_____

_____

_____

_____

_____

_____

_____

_____

_____

_____

_____

_____

_____

_____

_____

_____

_____

_____

_____

_____

_____

_____

Sample exam questions and answers with commentaries

Q1 Explain how a food handler can ensure that the food produced will be safe to eat.

Model answer

A food handler must make sure that their hands are always washed in hot, soapy water before and after handling any food. Handling food with dirty or contaminated hands can cause food poisoning. Food handlers must also shower daily and wear clean clothes. They must not cough or sneeze near food and not work when they are ill, especially if they have an upset stomach. Cross-contamination such as cutting raw chicken and then sandwiches using the same unwashed knife must not happen.

Food must be stored at the correct temperature, i.e. chilled foods at 5°C, frozen foods at -18°C and hot-held foods at a minimum of 63°C. All foods must be cooked to a core temperature of at least 75°C.

Commentary

This is a very good answer illustrating learned knowledge and understanding. Important points have been included such as cross-contamination and important temperatures. Marks from the high band would be awarded.

Weaker answer

They must wash their hands and make sure they wear clean clothes so they don't spread germs. If they are ill they mustn't attend work. They must work in a very clean fashion. Hot dinners must be kept warm and desserts must be kept in a fridge.

Commentary

This is a low band mark because each statement needs to use correct terminology and be qualified. For example, 'germs' are bacteria. Hot dinners must be kept HOT and never warm – warmth promotes bacterial growth. Should all desserts be stored in a fridge? What about hot apple pie?

Why mustn't an ill food handler attend work?

Q2 Describe the HACCP safety points a supermarket needs to follow when accepting a delivery of fresh fish and how it should be stored.

Model answer

The supplier of fresh fish must be reputable and trustworthy because this helps you know that the fish has been handled and stored safely. The fish must be delivered in a chiller van and the temperature of the fish must be at 5°C or below. There must be no damage to the packaging, especially no signs of 'mice bites', and the fish might be delivered on ice. All the fish should have plump flesh with scales intact, bright, glassy eyes and a fresh smell of the sea.

Fresh fish should be stored in a lidded container, with today's date on it, and immediately placed on the bottom shelf of the fridge at 5°C or colder. Ideally, the fresh fish will be stored in the 'fish' fridge to prevent any cross-contamination.

Commentary

This is a comprehensive answer that would access high band marks. The answer follows the HACCP in a logical way with each step being described and justified. Correct storage areas and temperatures are identified.

Weaker answer

You must put the fish into a fridge as soon as it is delivered. Make sure it looks OK and doesn't smell bad. Cover the fish or put it into a plastic box so it doesn't drip on other foods.

Commentary

This is a basic, low mark answer that hasn't justified the statements given. Each statement needs to describe both 'how?' and 'why?'.

SECTION 1

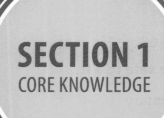

Target: I need to be able to understand and write about…

The meaning of food provenance

Food miles

The problems with food waste

FOOD PROVENANCE AND FOOD WASTE

How to prevent food waste

Food packaging and the environment

👍 Extra information may be found in the textbook pages 96–105.

Grade boost

Learn these key words and use them in your written work as this will show you understand the question:

Biodegradable
Carbon footprint
Environment
Greenhouse gases
Locally
Origin
Traceability

Why would you choose to buy local beef?

Food provenance

This simply means where the food is grown or the livestock reared. Knowing where the **origin** of the food is allows consumers to make informed choices and establishes **traceability**; i.e. should I buy **locally** reared beef rather than Argentinian beef or buy green beans from Peru instead of locally grown green beans? Local produce is usually fresher, may be a better quality and has a positive **carbon footprint**, which is why farmers' markets are so popular.

quickfire

1   Name an ingredient that is grown locally in your area.
2   Check your fridge to see how many countries the foods have come from.
3   What does the 'red tractor mark' found on some packaging mean?

Food miles

'Food miles' means the distance a food has had to travel to reach our kitchens. Locally grown runner beans may have travelled 6 miles, whereas runner beans from Zimbabwe have travelled 7600 miles. The carbon footprint of foods is calculated from the amount of fuel used during growing and production, transportation and the miles consumers have to travel to buy their shopping. The fewer the miles a food has travelled the better for the environment because less CO_2 has been produced.

quickfire

4 How can consumers reduce their food carbon footprint when shopping?

Amount of miles food travels to the UK ▼

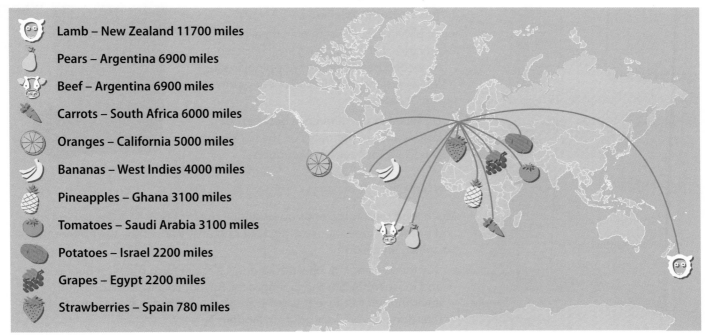

Lamb – New Zealand 11700 miles

Pears – Argentina 6900 miles

Beef – Argentina 6900 miles

Carrots – South Africa 6000 miles

Oranges – California 5000 miles

Bananas – West Indies 4000 miles

Pineapples – Ghana 3100 miles

Tomatoes – Saudi Arabia 3100 miles

Potatoes – Israel 2200 miles

Grapes – Egypt 2200 miles

Strawberries – Spain 780 miles

SECTION 1

8 WAYS TO REDUCE FOOD MILES

1 BUY LOCAL
Choose locally produced food. Buy food from the region if local food is not available. Even food produced within the UK is better than buying overseas food. Read food labels.

2 SHOP AT FARMERS' MARKETS
Good source of local seasonal foods available. Organic foods are often available.

3 GROW YOUR OWN VEGETABLES
Have your own vegetable patch. Vegetables and fruits you grow will not have created any food miles.

4 EAT SEASONALLY
Foods produced will be local to your area, e.g. swedes in winter. Plan meals around what is being harvested at the time.

5 PICK YOUR OWN
Go to a local farm, where you can pick almost anything from strawberries to garlic.

6 LEARN TO COOK FROM SCRATCH
Convenience foods are not often made locally. Convenience and cook–chill foods normally come from national food producers, which are then packaged for the individual stores.

7 WALK OR CYCLE TO THE SHOP
Avoid going by car if possible. Consider walking or cycling to the shop.

8 SHOP LESS FREQUENTLY
Shop once a week, or less if possible. Use stockpiling techniques, so you are never without the things you most often use. Create meals using these goods from scratch.

Food waste

Why is this topic so important?

- Many families waste £400–£700 worth of food each year because they buy too much for their needs. Most wasted food ends up in landfill sites producing **greenhouse gases**, which affect the **environment**.

- To prevent food waste plan meals in advance, use a shopping list, check what is needed before going shopping, freeze left-overs and use all foods before they go out of date.

- Understand the difference between 'best before' and 'use by' dates on the packaging, especially for cook–chill products.

Food packaging waste

Much food packaging ends up in landfill sites. It takes decades to degrade and produces greenhouse gases that negatively affect the environment. So, what can we do?

- Buy foods using minimal packaging, i.e. meat from the local butcher and loose fruit from the greengrocer. Buying locally is good for the environment because the items aren't pre-packed in sealed, plastic boxes that don't easily biodegrade in landfills.

- Buy fruit and vegetables using a local, seasonal 'box scheme'.

- Cooking from scratch rather than using ready-made meals produces far less packaging waste.

- Recycle all recyclable packaging waste.

- Reuse jars and plastic containers where possible.

Where should this waste go? ▼

quickfire

5   How could you use up these left-overs?

a) Stale bread

b) Mashed potato

c) Dry Victoria sandwich cake

d) 'Bendy' carrots

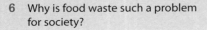

6   Why is food waste such a problem for society?

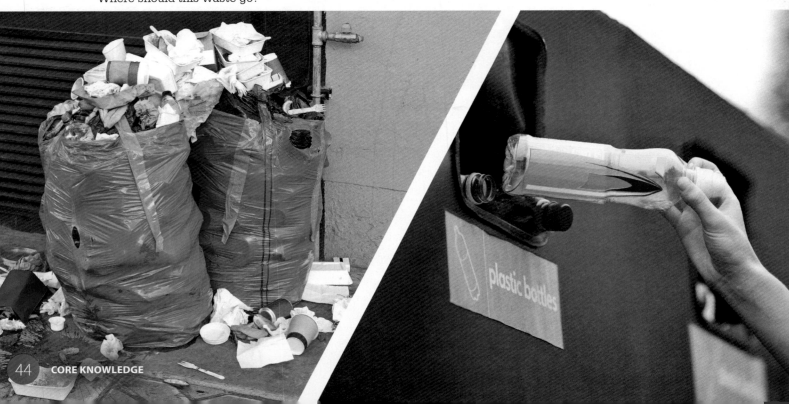

TYPES OF PACKAGING MATERIALS

PAPER AND CARDBOARD

- Cartons
- Bags
- Egg boxes
- Juice cartons
- Pizza boxes
- ✓ Biodegrade easily
- ✓ Cheap to produce
- ✓ Strong yet lightweight
- ✓ Can be printed on
- ✗ Not water resistant

GLASS

- Jars and bottles
- Jam jars
- ✓ Reusable
- ✓ Moisture proof
- ✗ Easily broken and is thus dangerous to handle

PLASTIC

- Bottles
- Trays
- Pots
- Ready-made meal containers
- Yoghurt pots
- Water bottles
- ✓ Easily recycled
- ✗ Is not **biodegradable**
- ✗ Must not be dropped as litter

METAL

- Aluminium
- Steel
- Cans
- Foil trays
- ✓ Recyclable

SECTION 1

REDUCE:

Avoid packaged products

Take reusable bags with you when shopping

REUSE:

Buy products that have refill packs, if available

Glass milk bottles are returnable

Use jars for storage or home preservations

RECYCLE:

Paper, cardboard, metal, glass and plastic

Take to recycling bank

Collected from home in recycling bins/boxes

quickfire

7 Why is recycling packaging better than sending it to landfill?

8 Which types of packaging are easily recyclable?

Grade boost

Identify the range of packaging materials used for sandwiches and wraps, and assess their suitability for use.

quickfire

9 Cook–chill foods have a short shelf life. Explain how this contributes to food waste.

EXAM QUESTIONS

1 Why is food sold in packaging?

_____

_____

2 Give two advantages of metal as a packaging material.

_____

_____

3 Explain the disadvantages of glass packaging.

_____

_____

4 Why should food provenance be considered when designing a new food product?

_____

_____

5 Explain the meaning of 'food sustainability'.

_____

_____

6 Discuss how families can reduce the amount of food waste they produce.

_____

_____

7 Why is reducing food waste cost effective?

_____

_____

_____

_____

8 What do you understand by 'food poverty'?

_____

_____

_____

_____

_____

9 How can consumers reduce their carbon footprint when buying foods?

_____

_____

_____

_____

_____

Sample exam questions and answers with commentaries

Q1 Explain how food manufacturers are responding to the public's environmental concerns.

Model answer

They can use less packaging on all products, e.g. sell fruit and vegetables loose or not double wrap individual items. Manufacturers are reducing their carbon emissions during processing and manufacture of products by using energy efficient machines and renewable energy by using solar panels. Most companies try to use packaging materials that are recyclable, biodegradable and/or compostable. Packaging is clearly labelled showing the origins of the food, which gives consumers options.

Commentary

A good, rounded answer, referencing packaging quantities and materials, provenance, energy efficiencies and renewables. It illustrates knowledge and some understanding. To get the top mark there should be examples given to several of the points made.

Weak answer

They are making packaging recyclable so that it doesn't have to go to landfill. Factories could install solar panels and wind turbines because this would reduce the amount of grid electricity used.

Commentary

This is a basic answer so could only access the lower band marks available. If justification had been given to the problems with sending packaging to landfill and the benefits to the environment of using energy from solar panels the student could gain more marks.

Q2 Describe different packaging materials that can be used to package food.

Model answer

Foods can be packaged in many different materials such as paper, foil, metal, card, plastic and glass.

Paper

Local shops often use paper bags for food, e.g. bakers may use them for rolls. Paper is good for the environment because it can be recycled but it isn't very strong and not waterproof so can easily get damaged.

Plastic

This comes in different types for food packaging. It could be cling film wrapped around a sandwich or a polystyrene pack of apples. Cling film is easy to use and is see-through so you can see what you are buying but it is flimsy. However, some councils don't recycle it. Rigid plastic boxes can be see-through, e.g. a beef joint in a plastic box or it can be coloured and have all sorts of information printed on it, e.g. ice-cream containers. This type of packaging is good because it is strong. It might be recyclable.

Cardboard

This is used to put all sorts of foods in like pizzas, burgers and biscuits in. Some foods will be wrapped in plastic first so that the board doesn't go soggy and disintegrate. Card or paperboard is lightweight, recyclable and it can have the company logo and details printed on it.

Commentary

This is a very good answer and would access the higher band marks. The candidate has identified the different types of packaging material and has described three types in some detail. Clear examples have been given for the use of each.

Weak answer

Foods can be put into all sorts of stuff like glass jars, paper bags, foil and tins. It must keep food safe so it doesn't get squashed. You couldn't have food just sat on a shop shelf. It must be wrapped up.

Commentary

The candidate has a very basic understanding of packaging. Several points have been made but they need further explaining and examples would be helpful. This response would receive low band marks.

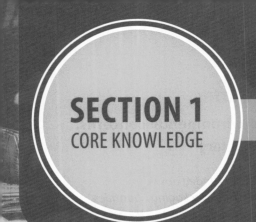

Target: I need to be able to understand and write about...

Climate

Geography

FACTORS INFLUENCING DIFFERENT CUISINES

Migration

Religion/faith/culture

Extra information may be found in the textbook pages 106–119.

Grade boost

Learn these key words and use them in your written work as this will show you understand the question:

| Climate | Culture | Traditions |
| Cuisines | Migration | |

▼ Which food is being harvested?

▼ Why is street food so popular?

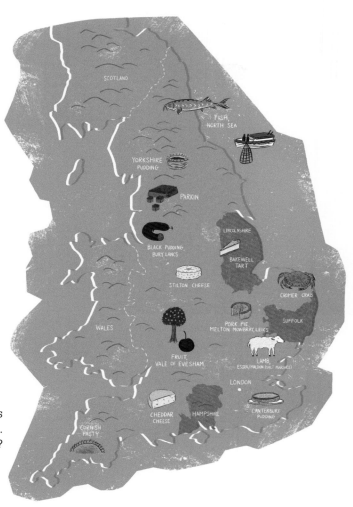

▲ Climate and geography influence the type of food products that are produced locally in both Wales (left) and England (right). Why is this the case?

Climate

The **climate** or weather is a controlling factor for what farmers can grow. If the ground is cold and hard or wet and sodden plants cannot be planted very easily. Most crops need some rain and warm weather to germinate and grow. Warm sunshine is needed to ripen plants and sweeten fruits.

Geography

The landscape of a region governs which crops and animals are raised for food. Flat land areas are needed for cereal production because combine harvesters could not effectively reap wheat grown on steep hills, whereas livestock can graze on the grass of very hilly land.

QUICKFIRE

1 Name two crops easily grown in each of the following regions:
   a) Scotland
   b) northern France
   c) southern Italy.

QUICKFIRE

2 Which crops are grown extensively on the plains of eastern England?

3 Wales, Dartmoor and the Lake District are famous for which food livestock?

Grade boost

Can you explain how a country's weather and landscape influence the crops that can be grown?

SECTION 1

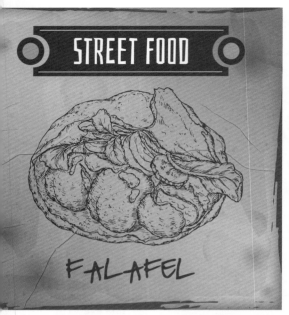

Street foods – embracing different cultures

Religion/faith/culture

People eat or avoid certain foods according to their religious instructions and beliefs, and **culture** and **traditions**.

- **Christians** Fish on Fridays, especially on Good Friday.

- **Jews** Foods must be 'kosher'. All pig/pork products are forbidden. Dairy foods and meat must not be cooked or eaten together. Separate pans used for milk/cheese only foods.

- **Muslims** Foods must be 'halal'. All pig/pork products are forbidden, as are shellfish and alcohol.

- **Sikhs** Beef, pork and alcohol are forbidden.

- **Hindus** Most follow a vegetarian diet and the cow is a sacred animal.

- **Buddhists** Follow a vegan/strict vegetarian diet with no alcohol taken.

- **Rastafarians** Most are vegetarians or vegans and only natural or 'pure' foods are eaten.

- **Seventh Day Adventists** Most are ovo-lacto vegetarian because meat is forbidden. Alcohol and caffeine are avoided.

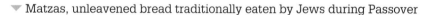

Matzas, unleavened bread traditionally eaten by Jews during Passover

quickfire

4 Suggest a two-course meal that can be eaten by:
a) Muslims
b) Jews
c) Buddhists.

Grade boost

Explain your understanding of kosher and halal processes.

Migration

Before the 1970s most families' dinners comprised some meat, potatoes and some vegetables, often in the form of stews. The fresh produce available in the shops was limited: rice was a milk pudding; cheese was mainly Cheddar; tomatoes were only available in the summer; and ingredients like pasta, garlic, noodles and peppers were rarely eaten and not easily available.

Nowadays, thanks to the immigrants who came to the UK in the 1970s bringing their national foods with them, we eat a very wide range of dishes that originate from all around the world.

▼ Muslim communities have introduced halal shops and food to the UK.

quickfire

5　How has **migration** affected the foods now eaten in the UK?

6　Identify one ingredient that is used extensively in **cuisines** from the following countries:

a) Italy

b) France

c) Greece

d) USA

e) Spain

f) Morocco

g) Thailand

h) Japan

i) South Africa.

▼ What street food might be being cooked here?

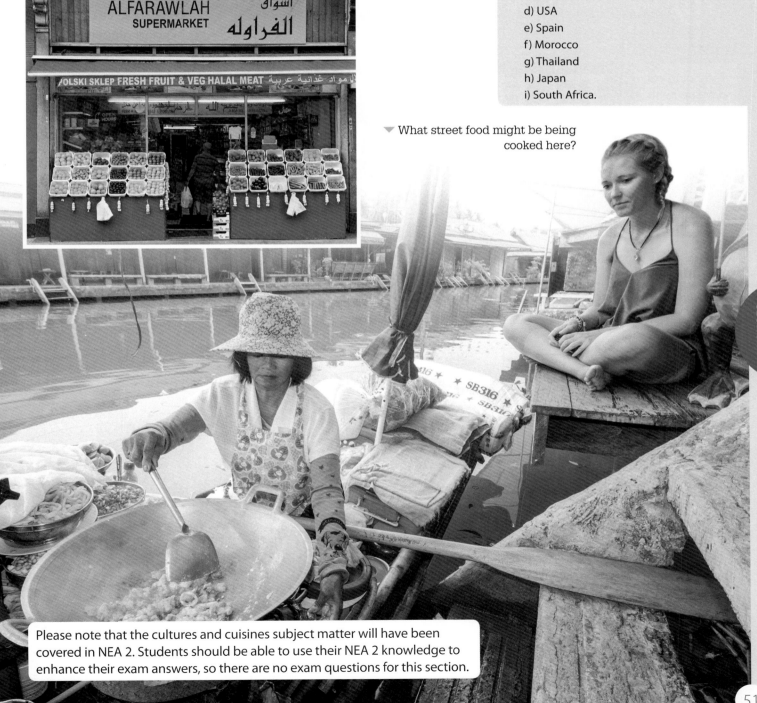

Please note that the cultures and cuisines subject matter will have been covered in NEA 2. Students should be able to use their NEA 2 knowledge to enhance their exam answers, so there are no exam questions for this section.

SECTION 1

51

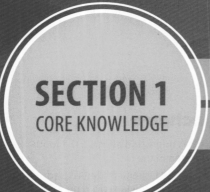

TECHNOLOGICAL DEVELOPMENTS

 Target: I need to be able to understand and write about...

Factors affecting food technology

Technological developments and health

TECHNOLOGICAL DEVELOPMENTS

How technological processing affects food

Food ingredients developments

Extra information may be found in the textbook pages 120–133.

Grade boost

Learn these key words and use them in your written work as this will show you understand the question:

Applications (apps)

Convenience foods

Fairtrade

Functional foods

Genetically engineered food

Genetically modified

High pressure processing (HPP)

Hydroponic

Insects

Mycoprotein

New food

Organic

Probiotic

Quick response codes (QR codes)

Sustainable

Factors affecting food technology

There are ELEVEN factors that push forwards changes in food technology.

1. **Population:** the more people there are, the more food is needed.

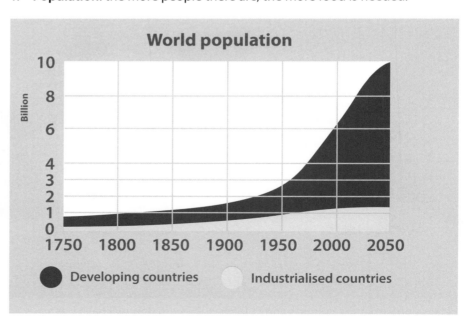

World population

Developing countries   Industrialised countries

▲ Global population increases

2. **Transport**: freezing and refrigerated transport have made the transportation of food easier.

3. **Preservation**: food preservation has been in use for hundreds of years (drying, freezing, canning, bottling, pickling, salting). More recently, people would rather eat fresh foods. New techniques have been developed that rely on heating and drying (modified atmosphere packaging (MAP) and **high pressure processing (HPP)**).

4. **TV, radio and social media**: influence customers about what they need or should buy. Some TV programmes highlight dietary diseases, encouraging the consumers to make positive dietary changes.

5. **Apps and barcodes**: **applications (apps)** make it easy to share information about products and to find out about products. Barcodes enable easy tracking of goods, while **quick response codes (QR codes)** can be scanned using a smartphone to gain information.

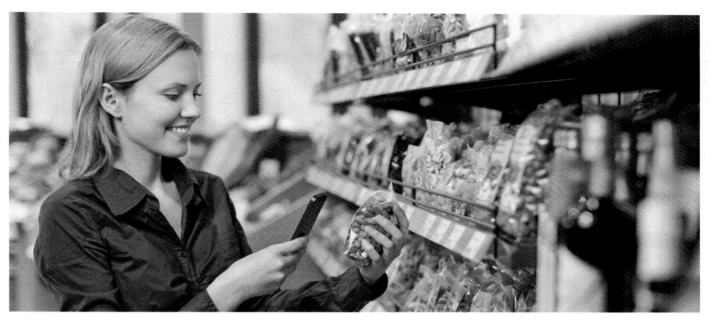

▲ Why is the customer using her phone?

6. **Environmental awareness**: consumers want to be able to reduce, reuse and recycle foods, packaging and fuel, and are buying **organic** and **sustainable** foods.

7. **Science**: constantly researching and developing techniques in food processing, food preservation and increased shelf life.

8. **Economics** (money): controls food companies' efficiencies to increase food shelf life, reduce food and packaging waste, and compete with other food companies. Demand for **Fairtrade**, assured food standards and Soil Association organic standards foods affect manufacturers' financial outgoings.

9. **Consumer demands**: affect food developments – changes in food 'fashions', population, culture and work/leisure time all change consumer demands. Concerns regarding the wellbeing and humane way animals are reared and slaughtered.

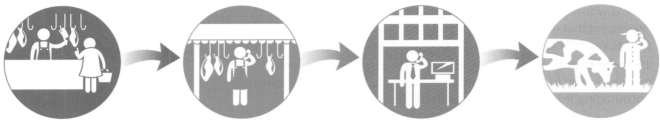

| Requests from consumers for specific product characteristics like grass-fed or organic | Retailers pass on request to packers to meet customer demands | Packers ask producers for livestock with desired characteristics of a specific stock | Producers raise animals to satisfy customer and consumer needs for a specific stock |

10. **Robots/automation:** used in food production. They are cheaper and more reliable than humans, can work 24/7, delivering uniform and consistent results.

Why does the food industry use automation? ▶

11. **Work/leisure time**: we now work longer hours, making our leisure time precious, so we don't want to spend hours preparing and cooking meals, preferring instead to rely on ready-made meals, **convenience foods** and take-aways.

These are the factors that you need to understand that lead to increasing popularity with convenience foods:

quicKfire

1 Learn three factors affecting food technology.
2 Can you explain each factor you've learned?

Grade boost

Describe three factors that have affected advances in food technology.

Make sure you understand what functional foods are.

How does 'Fairtrade' help farmers?

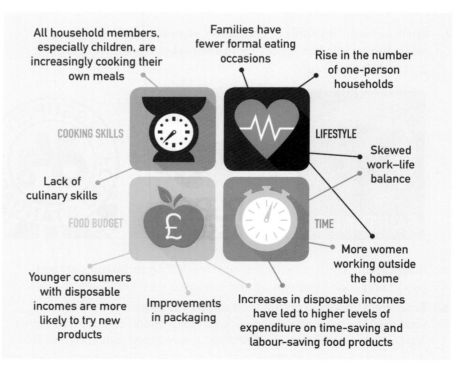

All household members, especially children, are increasingly cooking their own meals

Families have fewer formal eating occasions

Rise in the number of one-person households

COOKING SKILLS

LIFESTYLE

Lack of culinary skills

Skewed work–life balance

FOOD BUDGET

TIME

Younger consumers with disposable incomes are more likely to try new products

Improvements in packaging

Increases in disposable incomes have led to higher levels of expenditure on time-saving and labour-saving food products

More women working outside the home

Food ingredients developments

Food scientists can adapt the genetic composition of foods to:

- increase crop yields
- improve the nutrition of the food
- increase the shelf life of fresh produce.

In **genetically modified** (GM) or **genetically engineered foods** the DNA is changed so that the plant becomes resistant to disease and is therefore cheaper to produce. These changes would not usually occur 'naturally'.

'New' foods include textured vegetable protein (TVP) and **mycoprotein**, which are good sources of HBV protein and are widely used in vegetarian products. Seaweed is processed and incorporated into ready-made food products and dried **insects** are being considered for use in products because they are so nutrient rich.

Consumers receive additional or enhanced nutritional benefits from **functional foods** such as **probiotic** yoghurt, fat spreads and dairy foods where stanols and sterols have been added to lower blood cholesterol and eggs produced with richer levels of vitamin D and omega 3 fatty acids.

Some foods are fortified, with added vitamins or minerals, to either increase the nutritional profile, replace the nutrients lost during processing or add nutrients that aren't usually in the food, such as adding fibre to yoghurt.

▲ Would you eat fried insects?

▲ Cereals are often fortified with vitamins. Why would this be done?

quickfire

3 Can you state what the following terms mean?
   a) Genetically modified foods
   b) Genetically engineered foods
   c) 'New' foods
   d) Functional foods
   e) Fortified foods

4 Explain what the Eatwell Guide recommends you to eat.

5 Other than eating more healthily, research what advice the Change4Life initiative teaches us.

Technological developments and health

Government initiatives, such as the Eatwell Guide, five a day, Change4Life and healthy school meals help the consumer learn about diet, health and nutrition. This has led to food manufacturers creating 'healthier' food products such as low fat spreads/dairy foods and ready-made products and sugar-free or low calorie drinks and desserts. Manufacturers must include the nutritional information on all packaging of processed and ready-made products. This should help the consumer to make healthier choices.

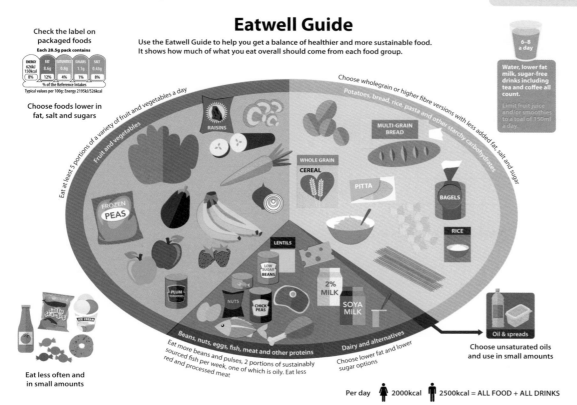

Eatwell Guide

Use the Eatwell Guide to help you get a balance of healthier and more sustainable food. It shows how much of what you eat overall should come from each food group.

Check the label on packaged foods

Each 28.5g pack contains

| ENERGY 626kJ 150kcal 8% | FAT 8.6g 12% | SATURATES 0.8g 4% | SUGARS 1.1g 1% | SALT 0.43g 8% |

% of the Reference Intakes
Typical values per 100g: Energy 2195kJ/526kcal

Choose foods lower in fat, salt and sugars

Eat at least 5 portions of a variety of fruit and vegetables a day

Fruit and vegetables

Choose wholegrain or higher fibre versions with less added fat, salt and sugar

Potatoes, bread, rice, pasta and other starchy carbohydrates

6–8 a day

Water, lower fat milk, sugar-free drinks including tea and coffee all count.

Limit fruit juice and/or smoothies to a total of 150ml a day.

Eat more beans and pulses, 2 portions of sustainably sourced fish per week, one of which is oily. Eat less red and processed meat

Beans, nuts, eggs, fish, meat and other proteins

Dairy and alternatives

Choose lower fat and lower sugar options

Oil & spreads

Choose unsaturated oils and use in small amounts

Eat less often and in small amounts

Per day ♀ 2000kcal ♂ 2500kcal = ALL FOOD + ALL DRINKS

EXAM QUESTIONS

1 State three reasons why foods are packaged.

[i] _____

[ii] _____

[iii] _____

2 Why is modified atmosphere packaging (MAP) good for preserving fresh foods?

_____

_____

_____

3 Describe, with examples, **hydroponic** food production.

_____

_____

_____

4 Discuss how functional foods can aid our diets.

_____

_____

_____

5 What is meant by food fortification? Give examples in your answer.

_____

_____

_____

6 What are the benefits of using automation by food manufacturers?

_____

_____

_____

_____

7 Why do consumers look for the red tractor, Fairtrade and the Soil Association labels on foods?

_____

_____

_____

_____

_____

8 Discuss how the changes to work and leisure time have affected the way we eat.

_____

_____

_____

_____

9 Explain how environmental factors affect food product developments.

_____

_____

_____

_____

_____

Sample exam questions and answers with commentaries

Q1 Discuss how the food industry has developed different types of food products to fit our changing lifestyles.

Model answer

Food manufacturers use technology to give perishable foods greater shelf life, which helps prevent food waste. There is a vast range of food products available to suit everyone, including vegetarians, vegans, Muslims and coeliacs. People now want to eat a wide range of foods due to going on foreign holidays and living in a multi-cultural society, so manufacturers produce foods from around the world; it is possible to eat Italian food one day and Thai the next.

Manufacturers produce products to suit different price bands such as value, own brand or branded products. This ensures customer's needs are met.

People live in a variety of households such as single people and widowed elderly, and the food industry has tapped into this to produce single portions of food, but they also produce family sized foods so the busy family doesn't have to cook from scratch, or multi-pack products so they don't have to visit the shops as often.

A new type of food is the breakfast cereal bar. People don't have time to sit and eat breakfast so they eat these bars while travelling to school or work.

Weaker answer

Manufacturers have a lot of technology to make loads of different foods. In the supermarkets, foods can be dear or cheap like Heinz beans or value beans. Some foods are family-sized and some foods are for one person. Like pies.

Commentary

This is a very well detailed answer showing both knowledge and understanding of the question. The only improvement could be that specific examples would underpin the statements made.

Commentary

Compare this answer to the model answer. You will see that the statements are correct but simplistic and could easily be expanded on. When writing an answer always ask yourself 'why?' and 'how?'.

Q2 Describe the costs involved in the design, development and manufacture of food products

Model answer

Before designing a new product the manufacturer needs to see if there is a gap in the market by using market research. If they don't do this the manufacturer could end up wasting both time and money designing a product that no-one will buy. Once it is decided to go ahead a prototype is made using a detailed specification. The company will need to employ highly skilled workers to do this, which is expensive. The company will need to invest in a computer system and probably CAD/CAM, which will add to the design costs. Once the prototype is made it needs to be sensory tested using the public.

Weaker answer

Once the food product goes into mass production there are many costs needed for staffing and equipment. A HACCP system is needed. Packaging needs to be designed, which is expensive. The business will have to advertise on TV, magazines and social media to get sales. If the product isn't properly costed the business could lose money and go bankrupt.

Commentary

A very good answer highlighting crucial design development considerations including need, costs and time, prototype and specification, skilled workers, CAD/CAM and sensory testing. The only improvement could be to include specific examples.

Commentary

This answer would be awarded low marks because the focus is only on the product once it goes to market, so they've not answered the question. There is no reference to the design and development stages needed before advertising a new product.

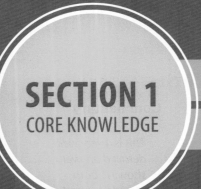

FACTORS AFFECTING FOOD CHOICE

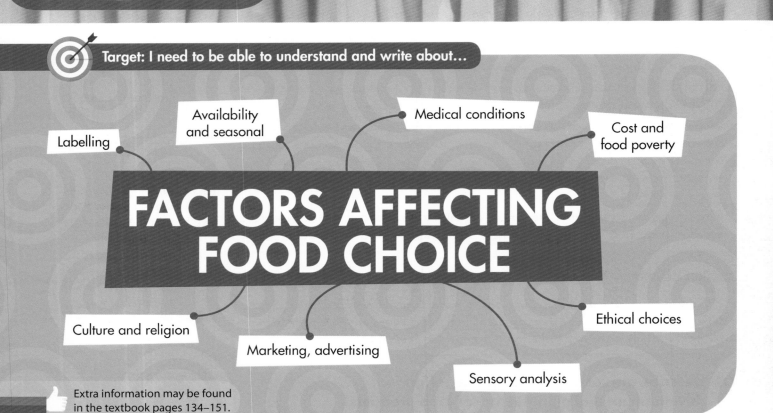

Target: I need to be able to understand and write about...

- Labelling
- Availability and seasonal
- Medical conditions
- Cost and food poverty

FACTORS AFFECTING FOOD CHOICE

- Culture and religion
- Marketing, advertising
- Sensory analysis
- Ethical choices

Extra information may be found in the textbook pages 134–151.

Grade boost

Learn these key words and use them in your written work as this will show you understand the question:

Advertising

Allergen

Allergy

Diabetics

Market research

Marketing

Pester power

Product placement

Availability and seasonalality

In the UK, supermarkets ensure that huge varieties of food are always available. They import products from around the world so we can readily buy 'out of season' foods such as strawberries and asparagus. In the 1960s and 1970s fruit and vegetables were only available when they were in season, for example tomatoes were only available in the summer months.

Ready-made and pre-prepared convenience foods are popular. They are ready to use or just need reheating and little effort or knowledge of food preparation is required.

SEASONAL FOOD

Fruit and vegetables that are grown in the UK through the year

Spring

March:
Rhubarb
Leeks

April:
Spinach
Sprouting broccoli

May:
Globe artichoke
Spring onions
Radishes

Summer

July:
Cherries, strawberries, tomatoes

June:
Peas
Gooseberries

August:
Redcurrants
Courgettes
Sweetcorn

Autumn

September:
Beetroot, pears, raspberries

November:
Kale, Brussels Sprouts

October:
Cax's apples
Maincrop potatoes
Onions
Pumpkins

Winter

December:
Swede
Turnips
Celery

January:
Parsnips
Winter radishes

February:
Spring greens
Celeriac

quickfire

1 Do you know when the following foods are in season in the UK?

a) Strawberries
b) Runner beans
c) Brussels sprouts
d) Leeks
e) Cox's apples
f) Plums

quickfire

2　Compare the cost of the following products:
a) 100g chickpeas
b) 100g lentils
c) 100g minced beef
d) 100g tinned tuna.

▲ Food, including rice and desserts, suitable for a Buddhist to eat

Grade boost

Find out if there are dietary rules for:
a) Christians　　c) Buddhists
b) Sikhs　　　　d) Rastafarians.

Food costs

Buying food is governed by how much money we have to spend. People on tight budgets may shop daily in street markets or low cost supermarkets and rely on buying cheaper protein foods such as pulses and tofu rather than meat and fish. People in food poverty may use food banks to tide them over.

Shop wisely by doing the following:

- plan your meals
- have a list of only what you need to buy and stick to it
- compare supermarket prices
- only buy foods on special offer if they are foods you usually use
- use vouchers and coupons
- buy foods with a good shelf life so that they don't get wasted.

Culture and religion

Our families' experiences and culture have a big impact on the foods we make and eat. So, if your mum or dad never cooked fish then you may not like to eat fish or if you were born to vegan parents then you may be a life-time vegan.

Many religions follow certain dietary rules:

 Christianity – fish is normally eaten on Fridays.

 Judaism – meat slaughtered according to kosher rules, pork and shellfish forbidden and meat and dairy must not be prepared, cooked or eaten in the same meal.

 Islam – meat slaughtered according to halal rules; pork and pork products forbidden.

 Hinduism – beef is not eaten and many Hindus follow a vegetarian diet.

Genetically modified food (GMF)

Scientists can now develop foods with altered genes to produce a specific outcome. Currently, the foods mainly concerned are tomatoes and maize. The main advantages are greater crop yields with greater disease resistance, and foods having a longer shelf life. However, many consumers worry about potential risks that may occur when interfering with nature.

Ethical choices

Many consumers are concerned about how their foods are produced, so choose to buy **organic**, farm assured, Fairtrade and low carbon footprint foods. Look for logos like the ones below:

quickfire

3 What is meant by the term 'organic foods'?
4 Can you explain what Farm Assured and Fairtrade mean?

Medical conditions

People with certain medical conditions have to be careful what they eat, for example **diabetics** need to control the amount of sugar they consume.

Some people have allergies and intolerances to certain foods, for example dairy or nuts, and need to be able to avoid consuming products containing the **allergen**.

quickfire

5 State three food allergens.
6 What is a milk intolerance called?

▲ Signs showing allergen-free products. Do you know which allergens they represent?

SECTION 1

61

Marketing and advertising

The food industry spends £ millions every year on **marketing** and **advertising** food products.

To identify the target market, food products undergo **market research**:

- **Primary** research involves taste testing and sensory analysis of existing or newly developed products.
- **Secondary** research is an analysis of existing information available.

Companies want supermarkets to place their products in prominent positions such as at the end of aisles, near the shop door and on shelves at eye level so the shoppers cannot miss them. This is called **product placement**.

Manufacturers and supermarkets encourage us to buy products using coupons, vouchers and special offers such as BOGOF (buy one get one free) or three for the price of two.

Grade boost

Describe three factors that influence the foods we buy.

How are new food products brought to market?

Make sure you can state how consumers can reduce their carbon footprint when buying food.

What does BOGOF stand for? ▶

quickfire

7 Explain the meanings of primary and secondary research and product placement.

8 How does 'pester power' sell products?

Food manufacturers and supermarkets spend enormous sums of money on advertising using TV, radio, social media, shop windows, newspapers and celebrity endorsement. Some advertisements for food and drinks, not high in fat and sugar, are aimed at children, which creates **pester power** when the children pester parents to buy the product.

All advertising is controlled by the Advertising Standards Agency (ASA) to make sure that all adverts are honest, truthful, legal and decent.

Labelling

Food labelling must show important information, including manufacturer's contact details, ingredients' list, weight or volume, nutritional profile, country of origin, any allergens in the product, and how to store and cook it. Labelling helps consumers make choices between similar products such as comparing how much fat per 100g there is in a branded lasagne and a 'value' lasagne.

Sensory analysis

Our food preferences depend on appearance, flavour, smell, texture and if we think we'd like it or not. You can train yourself to like food – you need to eat it at least ten times before you start liking it. We use the taste receptors on the tongue and air breathed in to taste the flavours of food.

Food manufacturers use sensory analysis to find out if people will like a product. In silence, groups of people will give written feedback about samples of food they have assessed according to appearance, smell, flavour and texture. This can be done through blind testing, ranking tests, triangle tests and rating tests.

Which type of cola is sugar-free? Circle your answer.

▲ Triangle test – typically used to test reactions to three identically labelled different products

Below are some examples of sensory descriptors.

Taste	Texture	Aroma	Appearance	Sound
Spicy	Moist	Sweet	Colourful	Crunchy
Bland	Soft	Yeasty	Dull	Sizzling
Sour	Juicy	Spicy	Shiny	Bubbling
Sweet	Crunchy	Citrus	Smooth	Popping
Salty	Chewy	Savoury	Rough	Fizzy
Fruity	Crisp	Buttery	Uniform	
Bitter	Smooth	Cheesy	Size	

The tongue and taste

The tongue is covered with thousands of very sensitive taste buds allowing you to experience sweet, salty, sour and bitter flavours.

Taste depends on your sense of smell. Try holding your nose and chewing raw onion. Can you taste it? That's why we can't taste food very well when we have a cold.

quickfire

9   What is the difference between blind testing, ranking tests and rating tests?

1 Discuss why some people buy and use only seasonal fruit and vegetables.

_____

_____

_____

_____

_____

2 What is the difference between an intolerance and an allergy?

_____

_____

_____

_____

_____

3 Describe **how** sensory analysis can be achieved when developing a new food product.

_____

_____

_____

_____

_____

4 Discuss why sensory analysis is important to the manufacturer.

_____

_____

_____

_____

_____

5 Why is market research vital to food manufacturers?

_____

_____

_____

_____

_____

_____

6 Describe the factors that affect the choices of foods we purchase?

_____

_____

_____

_____

_____

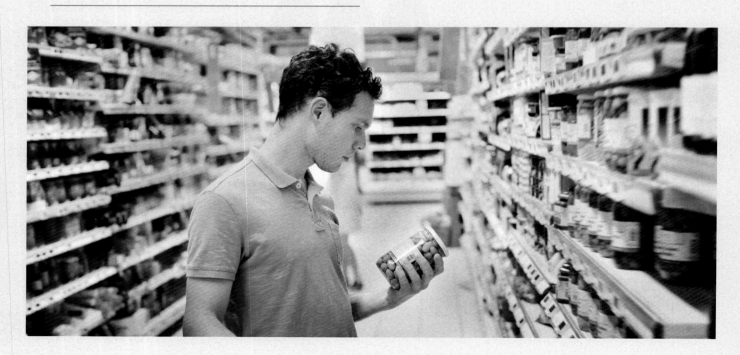

Sample exam questions and answers with commentaries

Q1 Why is the information on a food label important to the consumer?

Model answer

The law states that certain information must be on a food label. This helps the consumer know that the food is as stated, they can see the ingredients in the product and avoid it if necessary, e.g. someone on a reduced salt diet can see how much salt is in the product and reject it if it is high. Allergic customers can avoid buying a product if it contains allergens such as nuts or eggs.

The label must inform the customer how to store and cook the product. This is important so that the food is stored and cooked correctly to avoid getting food poisoning.

The packaging will also inform the customer if it can be recycled.

Commentary

This is a high band answer because the answer references the law, packaging information and why it helps the customer. Some examples have been given.

Weaker answer

So that the customer can see what's in the food, e.g. the package might say 'includes nuts' so a person with a nut allergy can avoid this product. The packaging will tell you what it is, e.g. chicken curry. The maker of the food must have their address on it.

Commentary

This answer would be a low mid-band mark response because it shows some understanding of the information needed on packaging. The first statement is justified, the second statement has an example and the third statement needs the reason: 'why?'

Q2 Explain why, over the years, the availability and supply of foods have changed.

Model answer

Food is easily imported these days due to good transport systems that have improved chilling storage systems. There are good road networks within the UK so that products can be easily and quickly moved around the country.

Improved advances in packaging technology such as modified atmosphere packaging (MAP) mean that the shelf life of ready prepared foods can be extended. Improved food additives also help improve shelf life. Customers are now aware of what is in the foods they buy and demand products that are low in fat, salt and sugar as well as being able to buy allergen-free products such as lactose-free milk and wheat-free bread rolls.

Commentary

This is a high band mark answer. It covers a range of reasoned points for the changes in food supply. Some good examples have been included.

Weaker answer

The foods we can buy have changed because manufacturers can make ready-meals in special packaging. They can fly certain ingredients from abroad so we can buy them. There is more food available.

Commentary

This is a very limited response that would access low band marks only. If the student had correctly explained the 'special packaging' or 'certain ingredients' mid-band marks could be awarded.

SECTION 1

65

BASIC MIXTURES AND RECIPES

Target: I need to be able to understand and write about…

What are high skills?

How will I get higher marks?

BASIC MIXTURES AND RECIPES

What happens if I just can't remember something in the exam?

Extra information may be found in the textbook pages 158–174.

What can go wrong with my cooking?

This section focuses on building your practical skills. To get those **higher marks** in NEA 2, the practical assessment, you need to be able to make three **high-skilled** dishes plus accompaniments. However, just because you've made high-skill dishes doesn't mean that you will automatically get the higher marks available, because the dish must be as near perfect as possible.

Let's take a lemon meringue pie as an example. The shortcrust pastry, baking blind, blended sauce and piped meringue are all high skills – so this is a really good dish to choose to show your skills. But, there are lots of things that can go wrong, as shown here.

Pastry edges are ragged.

Base has a bit of a soggy bottom.

Curd filling is too runny or too firm.

Lemon/sweetness balance isn't right.

Meringue has no volume.

Meringue is brown.

Pastry is too brown.

A lemon meringue pie pastry should be light, crumbly and melt-in-the mouth. The curd should taste lemony but not acidic and not too sweet. The meringue should be evenly piped, pale golden with a crunchy surface and 'mallowy' middle. Only then can you get the highest marks.

Can the practical assessment help me with the written exam?

Imagine that you are sitting in the exam hall trying to answer the exam paper and struggling to recall information because your mind has gone blank. Ask yourself *'What did I do in my practical assessment?'* because you might find the answer there.

For example, there's a question about raising agents and you think to yourself *'I haven't a clue!'* Well, you may be wrong. And this is where you need to have a conversation with yourself – in silence, of course, because it is the exam hall after all – which may go something like this:

That moment when your mind goes blank

Grade boost

Many of you should be able to achieve grade 8 or grade 9 for the final three dishes and accompaniments. But, to get these marks you need to show off your skills by illustrating high levels of competence and proficiency. The only way to perfect your skills is to practise, practise and practise again!

What have I made, in any practical session, where the dish had to rise?

I made cakes and bread rolls. But what made them rise? I'm going to make a list on the back page, here goes:

- Cakes need SR (self-raising) flour, baking powder and the eggs are whisked in.

- Swiss rolls need sieved flour and some serious egg + sugar whisking to hold air.

- Bread rolls use yeast. Yeast needs warmth, food, moisture, oxygen and time, then it will produce CO_2 making the dough expand and rise. But hot heat kills yeast.

You will suddenly remember vital information!

▲ What process is taking place here? What is the correct name for it and why is it important in food preparation?

HIGHER LEVEL SKILLS

What do I need to be able to prepare and cook?

quickfire

1   What are the proportions of fat to flour when making:
    a) shortcrust pastry
    b) flaky pastry?

quickfire

2   At what temperature does starch gelatinise?

Grade boost

Mix the cornflour into a paste with a little water **before** adding it to the sauce liquid.

quickfire

3   What is the difference between cornflour and plain flour?

quickfire

4   Which cut of beef would you use for a casserole?
5   Name three garnishes you could use for a fish pie.

PASTRIES

Fats sold in plastic tubs are too soft for making pastry so always use hard 'block' fats. Good shortcrust pastry should be thin, crumbly and 'melt-in-the-mouth', and not be chewy.

ROUX BASED SAUCES

Roux based sauces include béchamel and cheese sauces. This skill illustrates gelatinisation. Make sure the starch is cooked out before serving to avoid it tasting 'gritty'. Blended sauces, for example custard and lemon meringue pie filling, use cornflour to thicken them.

MERINGUE

When making a meringue, add 2–3 drops of vinegar or lemon juice to the egg white before whisking for it to be successful. Avoid using even slightly greasy mixing bowls and beaters because the egg whites won't foam.

MEAT AND FISH – BONING AND FILLETING

This includes boning chicken legs and thighs, scraping chop bones clean and gutting and filleting fish. Use a very sharp knife to follow the line of the bone in the meat. Make sure the fish scales have been removed before cooking.

DECORATED CAKES AND GATEAUX

Cakes and gateaux can be decorated with just about anything you wish. The decorations can be edible, for example chocolate chips on a chocolate cake or lemon and orange slices on an orange gateau, or purely decorative, for example a piece of holly on a Christmas cake.

quickfire

6   State two different types of icing.
7   State the method used to make a Swiss roll.
8   What would you use to decorate a coffee gateau and a summer fruit roulade?

RICH OR SHAPED YEASTED DOUGHS

A yeasted dough is used to make cinnamon rolls, doughnuts, soft dinner rolls and sticky buns to name a few. It is a rich dough, which has higher fat and sugar content than normal dough. This creates softer breads.

Grade boost

Add slightly more water than the bread recipe says to make sure the dough isn't 'tight'. You can always add more flour to a wet or sticky dough but you can't add more water to a 'tight' dough. A 'tight' dough has enough water to hold the ingredients together to form a lump of dough but not enough water so that you can stretch it for kneading.

quickfire

9   What is the difference between a standard bread dough and a rich dough?

SHAPED PASTA

Home-made shaped pasta includes ravioli and cannelloni. Knead the pasta dough for a good ten minutes before letting it rest for 20 minutes. Pasta should be served 'al dente' and not soft and squidgy. Place pasta in salted, **rapidly boiling water** (rolling boil) and cook for 2–3 minutes.

COMPLEX ACCOMPANIMENTS AND GARNISHES

Complex accompaniments and garnishes, include fanned strawberries, chocolate whirls and shards or spun sugar. Practise these because they are really quick and easy to do and give your food a professional finish.

Grade boost

Melt sugar in a pan over a high heat – keep swirling the pan until a golden colour forms.

Melt chocolate in a microwave oven using low power. Check it every 5–10 seconds. Ideal temperature is 32°C.

MEDIUM LEVEL SKILLS

What do I need to be able to prepare and cook?

Grade boost

When making puff pastry, if the rolling out goes wrong don't screw it all together and re-roll because you will lose all the puffy layers. Simply fold the pastry on top of itself and re-roll.

quickfire

10 What is the difference between carrot batons and carrot julienne?

Grade boost

Carefully fold the whisked egg white into the rest of the ingredients to keep the airy volume.

quickfire

11 What is the term for an aerated egg mix?
12 Which ingredient can be added to cheesecakes to help them set?

READY-MADE PUFF PASTRY DISHES

If you have to use ready-made puff pastry buy the block of pastry and roll it out and shape it. You will then be showing some skill.

KNIFE SKILLS

Evenly cut vegetables and fruit dishes to show good knife skills. Use a sharp knife and place a damp dishcloth under the board to prevent accidents. Practise different veg cuts at home so that in the practical session you will be able to dice, slice, baton or julienne your vegetables really quickly.

CHEESECAKES AND MOUSSES

When making cheesecakes or mousses in a practical, make these first and in individual rings or dishes so that they will set within the time. To look good these dishes need brightly coloured decorations, usually fresh fruit.

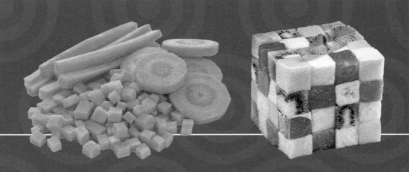

WINE SAUCES AND REDUCTIONS

These are simple sauces that add moisture and extra flavour to a meal. Always taste sauces and adjust the seasoning before serving.

quickfire

13 Can you describe how to make a reduction?

CAKES, BISCUITS AND SCONES

These are generally served for afternoon tea or as a snack rather than with a two-course meal. However, small, neat biscuits are an excellent accompaniment to creamy desserts such as panna cotta or crème brulée. A batch of cakes or biscuits should all be the same size as each other.

quickfire

14 What method of baking would you use to make 12 fairy cakes?

15 Why are biscuits still soft when you take them out of the oven?

BASIC BREADS

These include loaves of bread, batches of bread rolls or pizza bases. See the 'rich' dough 'Grade boost' for more information.

quickfire

16 What conditions does a yeasted dough need to 'grow'?

BASIC LEVEL SKILLS

What do I need to be able to prepare and cook?

quickfire

17 Which ingredients are used for a crumble topping?

18 Name three different types of bread to make sandwiches with.

quickfire

19 What could you serve with a pizza?

20 Which herb is shown on this pizza?

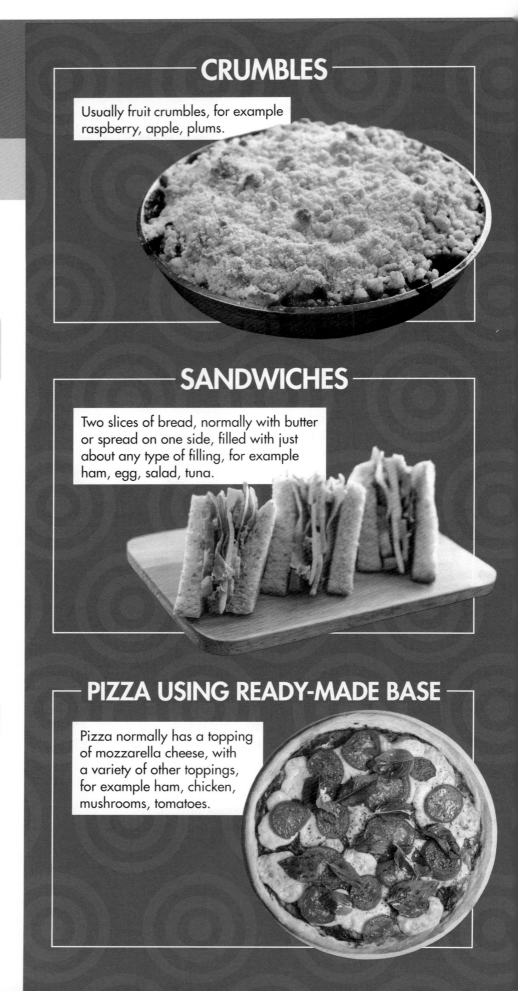

CRUMBLES

Usually fruit crumbles, for example raspberry, apple, plums.

SANDWICHES

Two slices of bread, normally with butter or spread on one side, filled with just about any type of filling, for example ham, egg, salad, tuna.

PIZZA USING READY-MADE BASE

Pizza normally has a topping of mozzarella cheese, with a variety of other toppings, for example ham, chicken, mushrooms, tomatoes.

FILLED JACKET POTATOES

These can be filled with just about anything you fancy, for example baked beans, cheese, curry, tuna, or a mixture of any of these.

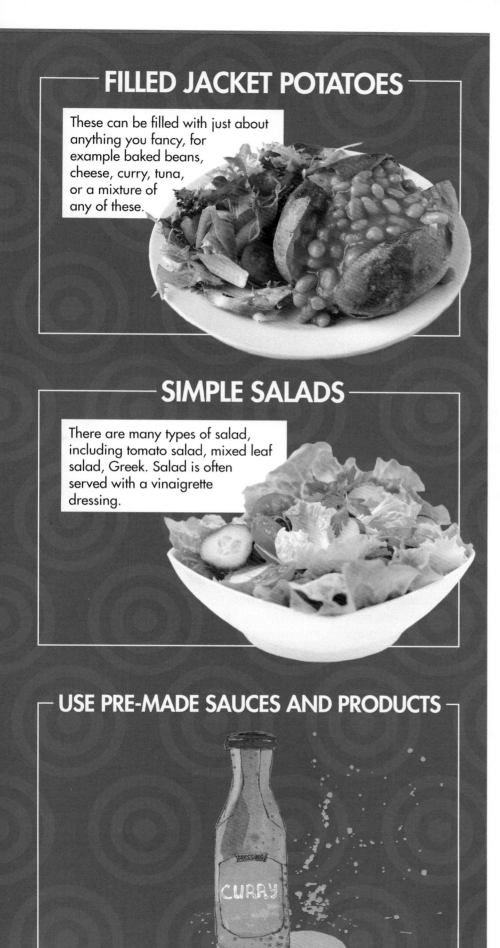

SIMPLE SALADS

There are many types of salad, including tomato salad, mixed leaf salad, Greek. Salad is often served with a vinaigrette dressing.

USE PRE-MADE SAUCES AND PRODUCTS

Grade boost

The more complex and 'tricky' a dish is to make the higher the skill level it will be. Then it is down to you to make the dish proficiently. Part of learning to cook is to learn ingredient ratios and basic recipes, then you can cook without using recipe books.

	Type	Proportions/ratios
Cakes	Creamed and all-in-one	Equal weight of eggs, butter, sugar, SR flour
	Whisked sponge	Equal weights of eggs, sugar & flour
Pastry	Shortcrust	½ hard fat to flour
	Flaky/rough puff	¾ hard fat to flour
	Suet	½ suet to SR flour
	Choux	2/50/60 = 2 eggs, 50g butter, 60g flour
Roux sauce	Pouring	25/25/500 = 25g each fat and flour, 500ml liquid
	Coating	50/50/500 = 50g each fat & flour, 500ml liquid
	Panada	100/100/500 = 100g each fat and flour, 500ml liquid

So, once you know that shortcrust pastry is half fat to flour you never need to look it up ever again!

quickfire

21 What are the ingredient ratios for a standard creamed cake?

Target: I need to be able to understand and write about…

CEREALS

- What are cereals?
- Processing wheat
- Cooking cereals
- Nutrition and diet
- Food poisoning in cereals
- Provenance (where cereals come from)
- Safe storage of cereal products
- Science of cereals during cooking

Extra information may be found in the textbook pages 176–184.

quickfire

1 Why are staple foods so important for:
  a) the developing world
  b) low-waged or low-income families?

Grade boost

Learn these key words and use them in your written work as this will show you understand the question:

Bran
Endosperm
Germ
Milled
Primary processing
Secondary processing
Staple food
Starchy carbohydrate
Wholegrains

What are cereals?

Cereals are edible grasses grown and harvested for their grain. They are a popular food source and, often, are the main source of food in a diet, making them a **staple food**. Popular cereals include wheat, rice, oats, maize and barley. However, rye, millet, buckwheat, quinoa, sorghum and amaranth are gaining popularity. In the UK wheat is a staple food, whereas in China rice is the staple food.

A wheat grain ▲

▼ Wheat   ▼ Rice   ▼ Oats

▲ Maize   ▲ Barley

Provenance

Wheat is one of the main cereal crops grown in the UK. The map on the right shows the main wheat-growing areas in the UK.

Processing wheat

Wheat is **milled** to make flour and is an example of **primary processing** – milling is the crushing of the wheat grain to separate the **bran**, **germ** and **endosperm**. After the wheat grain has been milled to make flour it can then be processed for a second time (called **secondary processing**) to make a range of food products such as biscuits, cakes, sauces, bread, pasta, pizza bases, pies and breakfast cereals. Organic wheat is grown and processed following strict Soil Association rules.

Wheat is also processed to make the following different types of cereal:

- **Wheat bran** – biscuits, muffins, bread, breakfast cereals
- **Puffed wheat** – breakfast cereal and snack bars
- **Kibbled wheat** – mixed grain bread
- **Semolina** – pasta, cakes
- **Couscous** – served with mains and in salads
- **Bulgar wheat** – soup, burgers, casseroles.

Safe storage of cereal products

Dried cereal products have long shelf lives if kept airtight. However, 'wet' cooked cereal products such as sauces, gravies, rice puddings, rice and pasta salads must be treated as high-risk foods because **bacillus cereus** reproduces quickly. To prevent food poisoning, they must be stored at 5°C, reheated to above 75°C and eaten within a day or two of making. Baked cereal products, for example bread, cakes, biscuits and pastry, go mouldy quickly so need to be stored in containers.

Cooking cereals

Cereals need to be cooked.

- When cooked in a liquid they will soften, creating a gel that thickens the liquid, for example cheese sauce and stews.
- When cooked in a dry heat they will create golden brown dextrins on the surface of the food, for example bread and pastry.

■ Main wheat-growing areas of the UK

quickfire

2   Draw and label a wheat grain.
3   Name three foods that contain wheat.

Cheese and spinach scones ▼

Science of cereals during cooking

Cereals undergo a physical change when heated:

- Moist heat gelatinises the starch in flour.
- Dry heat creates dextrins in baked wheat products.
- Heat causes the wheat proteins to coagulate, which help to set a product.

Nutrition and diet

Cereals contain lots of **starchy carbohydrate**, B vitamins and low levels of protein. However, wholegrains – 100% grain with nothing removed – have higher nutritional values than processed cereals and contain some healthy fats, NSP/dietry fibre (soluble and/or insoluble) and vitamins B and E. Eating **wholegrains** may help to reduce the risk of heart disease and type 2 diabetes, and assist in controlling blood cholesterol levels.

quickfire

4   Can you explain how the grains of wheat become bread?

▲ Ears of wheat, grains of wheat and varieties of bread

quickfire

5   Name three cereals.

6   How would you store cereals at home?

Food poisoning in cereal foods

All harvested cereals must be kept dry and cool to prevent bacteria, yeasts, moulds and fungi from growing. The storage areas must be clean and free from pests such as beetles, birds, rats and mice because these can contaminate the cereals with Weil's disease, Salmonella and listeria.

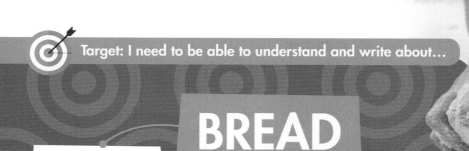

Target: I need to be able to understand and write about…

BREAD

What is bread?

How to make bread

The function of yeast in bread-making

👍 Extra information may be found in the textbook pages 185–191.

▲ Kneading dough for bread

What is bread?

Bread is a staple food in much of the world. It is made from strong flour, yeast, salt and water. Fat is often added to extend the shelf life of bread, while sugar can be used for sweetness and to add colour.

How to make bread

Bread made the traditional way can take about four hours to make. In the 1960s a faster, mechanical method of making bread was devised, which is used today by all mass production bakeries. This is known as the Chorleywood process and a loaf of bread can be made in about 90 minutes. The dough has vitamin C added to it and has to be vigorously kneaded in high-speed mixers.

The function of yeast

Yeast is used in **leavened** bread making. It will produce CO_2 when it is activated by the water in the dough, 'fed' by the flour and the oxygen during kneading, and then kept in a warm environment. The CO_2 bubbles make the dough rise to create the risen, light and airy texture of bread. Yeast is killed by too much salt, sugar and heat.

Not all bread is leavened, which means that no raising agent is used. These breads, which are **unleavened**, tend to be flat and a bit chewy such as tortillas, roti and matzos.

quickfire

7   Describe WHY these ingredients are needed when making bread:
a) strong flour   b) yeast   c) water   d) salt.

quickfire

8   State the conditions that yeast needs to produce CO_2.
9   a) List the seven steps of bread-making.
b) What are the benefits to the manufacturer of the Chorleywood process?
10   Why do products such as tortillas and matzos benefit from not being leavened?

Grade boost

Learn these key words and use them in your written work as this will show you understand the question:
Leavened
Unleavened

▲ Tortillas are an unleavened bread

Grade boost

You must show you understand the following:
- How each ingredient works.
- The importance of gluten formation.
- What happens at each stage of bread-making.
- Why coeliacs should avoid gluten products.

Target: I need to be able to understand and write about...

PASTA

Pasta is extruded into a wide range of shapes such as strands, shells, sheets and spirals.

It is a convenient, staple food in the UK due to easy availability and because when dried it has a long shelf life

Pasta is made from flour with a strong gluten content; it is kneaded with egg for 10 minutes until it is silky and smooth.

It is quick and easy to cook. Simply place in rapidly boiling salted water and cook until **al dente**. Cooked pasta should never be soft.

 Extra information may be found in the textbook pages 192–194.

Grade boost

Learn this key word and use it in your written work as this will show you understand the question:

Al dente

Making tagliatelle with a pasta machine

Cooked rice and pasta

Bacillus cereus, found in all cereal products, can survive high cooking temperatures, producing spores which increase the risk of food poisoning from eating rice and pasta salads. Reheating cooked rice can be risky too.

Use 'Salmonella free' eggs when making fresh pasta to avoid the risk of food poisoning.

quickfire

11 Explain why the shape of the pasta indicates the type of sauce that is best served with it.

12 a) What does al dente mean?

b) Why is wholemeal pasta better for you than white pasta?

▼ Can you name the different pasta shapes?

Grade boost

Can you describe how bacterial spores are formed?

How would you know that eggs are Salmonella free?

Target: I need to be able to understand and write about...

BREAKFAST CEREALS

Many cereals are processed and made into breakfast cereals. Most commonly: wheat, maize (corn), oats and rice.

Frequently, they are fortified with vitamins and minerals to add to nutritional value.

Some have sugar and salt added to them, which makes them less healthy.

The cereals are processed in different ways, including: puffed, shredded, flaked and rolled.

They are often mixed with other ingredients (nuts, dried fruit or honey) to improve their flavour and nutritional value.

Extra information may be found in the textbook page 195.

▼ Can you identify these breakfast cereals?

RICE

There are many varieties of rice grown, mainly in Asia where it is a staple food.

During cooking, rice grains soften, swell and absorb the cooking water.

Rice harvest and processing is very similar to that of wheat. A grain of rice is also similar in make-up to a grain of wheat.

Rice is a good source of starchy carbohydrate, B vitamins and low levels of protein. Wholegrain rice is a good source of NSP/dietary fibre.

Cooked rice is a high-risk food due to bacillus cereus – cooked rice dishes must be stored at 5°C and eaten within a day or two of cooking.

As well as being served with curry, chilli con carne or in sweet puddings, rice can also be processed into rice flour, rice starch and rice wine.

Rice, like pasta, is very quick and easy to cook. Simply cook in fast boiling, salted water until al dente.

 Extra information may be found in the textbook pages 196–199.

Think!

Countries that often experience serious flooding or earthquakes are usually given food aid in the form of rice. What are the health issues that may result from a diet comprising mainly of rice?

▼ What crop are these people harvesting?

Research how long it takes to cook brown rice and white rice. ▼

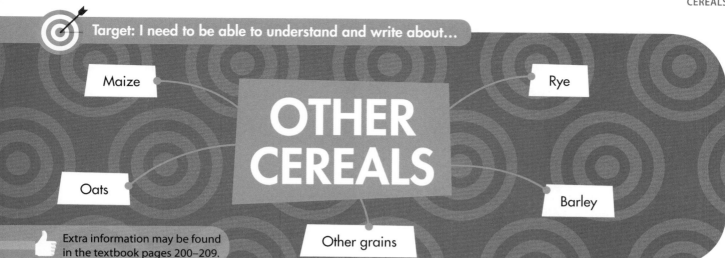

Target: I need to be able to understand and write about...

Maize

Rye

OTHER CEREALS

Oats

Barley

Other grains

Extra information may be found in the textbook pages 200–209.

MAIZE

Commonly called sweetcorn. This is a staple food in the USA, South America and Asia. It can be eaten as a vegetable or in a flour form (cornflour), used to thicken liquids. There is no gluten in maize, making it suitable for **coeliacs**. However, it cannot be used to make successful bread, cakes and pastries. The nutritional profile is similar to all cereals. Communities who rely on maize as a staple food can become deficient in niacin and develop **pellagra**.

OATS

Grown in cool climates in the northern hemisphere. They are used mainly for breakfast cereals and cereal bars. Their nutritional profile is similar to all other cereals but oats also contains soluble NSP/dietary fibre, which has been proven to reduce blood cholesterol, which is a benefit to human health.

BARLEY

The second most widely grown crop in the UK. Pearl barley is often used as a thickening agent.

RYE

Rye flour makes dense, dark, chewy breads that are widely eaten in Germany and Scandinavia.

Grade boost

Learn these key words and use them in your written work as this will show you understand the question:

Coeliac

Gluten

Pellagra

Grade boost

Can you explain the difference between soluble and insoluble NSP/dietary fibre?

Other grains include:

TAPIOCA

Used in milky puddings as well as a thickener in soups and stews.

SAGO

Used in milky puddings.

SORGHUM

A cereal grain that is milled into flour and used to make flatbreads. It is gluten free.

ARROWROOT

Used to thicken sauces but has the advantage of becoming clear once cooked. This makes it a good glaze on fruit.

QUINOA

A seed that is a good source of all the essential amino acids making it a high biological protein and widely used in vegan diets. It is prepared and used in a similar way to rice.

1   Name the three parts of the wheat grain.

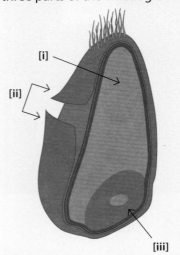

[i] _____

[ii] _____

[iii] _____

2   Name two nutrients found in most cereals.

[i] _____

[ii] _____

3   State two types of cereal other than wheat.

[i] _____

[ii] _____

4   What are the benefits to a bread manufacturer of using the Chorleywood process?

_____

_____

_____

_____

5   How can you increase the dietary fibre/NSP content of bread rolls?

_____

_____

_____

_____

6   Why is strong flour used to make pasta?

_____

_____

_____

_____

7   Identify three cereal based foods that show:

a)   gelatinisation

b)   dextrinisation

c)   coagulation.

[a] _____

[b] _____

[c] _____

8   Explain how yeast causes bread to rise.

_____

_____

_____

_____

9   State two changes that occur when bread is toasted.

[i] _____

[ii] _____

Sample exam questions and answers with commentaries

Q1 Describe how flour can thicken a sauce.

Model answer

When starch is heated in a liquid the starch granules soften and gradually absorb the liquid. The soft, swollen starch granules absorb more and more liquid causing the liquid to thicken. This is called gelatinisation and occurs at about 60°C.

Commentary

Highest band marks because the answer shows correct understanding of the gelatinisation process. Correct terminology has been used.

Weak answer

Boil flour and milk together to get a thick sauce. You can stir in some cheese and pour it onto cauliflower to make cauliflower cheese.

Commentary

*This is a very limited answer because the first sentence needs expanding. What is it in flour that 'thickens'?
No reference to softening starch granules, absorption of liquid, specific temperature or the term 'gelatinisation'.*

Q2 Explain why the Chorleywood process is a quicker way of making bread.

Model answer

The Chorleywood method of making bread is quicker because the dough uses hard fats, extra yeast and vitamin C, which are then kneaded very fast by machines. The elastic, gluten structure is allowed to develop more quickly making the bread dough ready to bake in a much shorter time than traditionally made bread. This method also produces a softer texture bread that doesn't go stale as quickly.

Commentary

Highest band mark because the answer shows correct understanding. There is reference to it being a faster method, using the addition of vitamin C. There is also reference to gluten, softer texture and longer keeping qualities.

Weak answer

This method makes bread much faster because machines are used.

Commentary

A very basic answer that would get one mark because of the reference to bread being faster to make and made using machinery. It doesn't show much recall knowledge or any understanding of the Chorleywood process.

 Target: I need to be able to understand and write about...

Herbs and spices

Vegetarian diets

Classification and types

Seasonality

FRUIT AND VEGETABLES

Nutritional values and health benefits

Preservation of fruit and vegetables

Science of fruit and vegetables

Why fruit and vegetables are cooked

Processing and preparation

How to choose, prepare and cook vegetables

Extra information may be found in the textbook pages 214–237.

Grade boost

Learn these key words and use them in your written work as this will show you understand the question:

Enzymic browning

Mirepoix

Classification and types of fruit and vegetables

All fruits and vegetables come from plants that are grown in the ground. Not all parts of each plant are eaten.

The fruit is the part of the plant that holds the seeds, which will form new plants.

quickfire

1   State two examples of a fruit or vegetable used from each plant part shown in the diagram on the right.

flower   leaf

pea pod

stem

ground level

root

Parts of the pea plant growing above and below ground ▶

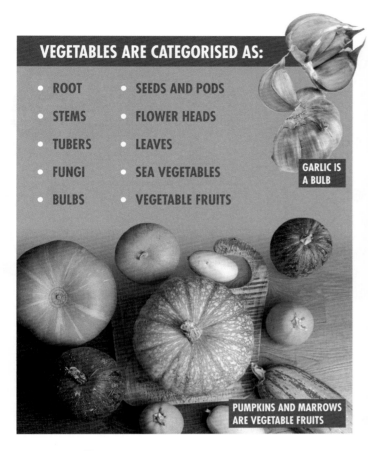

VEGETABLES ARE CATEGORISED AS:

- ROOT
- STEMS
- TUBERS
- FUNGI
- BULBS
- SEEDS AND PODS
- FLOWER HEADS
- LEAVES
- SEA VEGETABLES
- VEGETABLE FRUITS

GARLIC IS A BULB

PUMPKINS AND MARROWS ARE VEGETABLE FRUITS

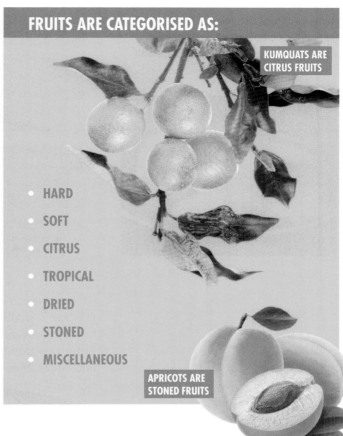

FRUITS ARE CATEGORISED AS:

KUMQUATS ARE CITRUS FRUITS

- HARD
- SOFT
- CITRUS
- TROPICAL
- DRIED
- STONED
- MISCELLANEOUS

APRICOTS ARE STONED FRUITS

quickfire

2 State two examples of a fruit from each of the above categories.

Nutritional values and health benefits

A balanced diet will contain at least **five portions** of fruit and vegetables eaten daily. This is because some nutrients, such as vitamin C and dietary fibre/NSP, are found **ONLY** in fruit and vegetables so a diet lacking in fruit and vegetables can cause nutritional deficiencies and health problems. Different fruit and vegetables contain varying amounts of each nutrient, which is why a range must be eaten.

- Carbohydrates are found in starchy, root vegetables and sweet fruits.
- Vitamin A is found in many yellow and orange vegetables and fruits.
- Vitamins C is found in citrus fruits, berries, peppers, tomatoes and some green vegetables.
- Dietary fibre/NSP is found in all fruit and vegetables but excellent sources are leeks, berries, figs and peas.

◀ Berries are good sources of dietary fibre/NSP.

quickfire

3 Name two fruits that are rich in vitamin A.
4 State three carbohydrate-rich vegetables.
5 Why is it better to eat a jacket potato and its skin than boiled potatoes?

The health benefits of these nutrients are immense:

CARBOHYDRATES — Energy

VITAMIN A — See in dim light

VITAMIN C — Heals skin cells

DIETARY FIBRE/NSP — Prevents constipation

An easy way to eat a wide range of fruit and vegetables is to 'eat a rainbow' – make sure that your plate is one-third filled with very colourful fruit and vegetables. Ideally, we should eat **five portions** a day: having more vegetables than fruit. You can have fresh, canned or frozen fruit and vegetables.

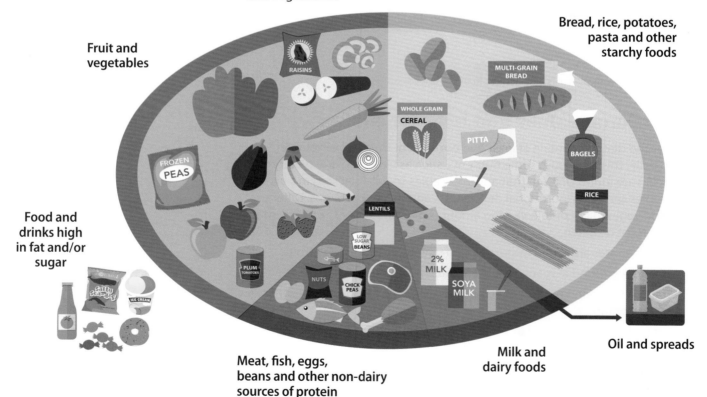

Fruit and vegetables

Bread, rice, potatoes, pasta and other starchy foods

Food and drinks high in fat and/or sugar

Oil and spreads

Meat, fish, eggs, beans and other non-dairy sources of protein

Milk and dairy foods

▲ Fruit and vegetables are important to include in your diet, as shown in the Eatwell Guide.

Fruit and vegetables are best eaten when they are in **season** because they taste better and are richer in some nutrients, and they should be eaten when they are as fresh as possible. The nutrients in fruit and vegetables are destroyed through damage from cutting, heat and water from cooking, and oxygen in the air.

Science of fruit and vegetables

Enzymes, oxygen and naturally occurring moulds and yeasts cause spoilage and decay of fruit and vegetables.

Yeasts and moulds feed on the moisture and sugar of fruit and vegetables making them soft, mushy and discoloured. They will then look, smell and taste unpleasant.

Apples, pears, parsnips, potatoes, bananas and avocados go brown, grey or black once peeled, sliced or grated. This is due to **enzymic browning** which is a reaction between the plant cell enzymes and oxygen. To prevent enzymic browning the fruit and vegetables must be treated in some way, for example covered with water/water + lemon juice, blanched or cooked immediately.

Fruit and vegetables that contain natural sugars will caramelise when cooked. As the plant cells are heated, the natural sugars turn into caramel, browning the food. Examples are fried onions and bananas.

Starchy vegetables, such as potatoes, can thicken a liquid through gelatinisation. When the starch cells in the potato are heated they will soften and absorb some of the surrounding liquid. To thicken a casserole or stew simply place diced potato into the gravy and continue cooking. The potato will absorb some of the liquid, creating a thicker gravy.

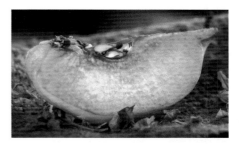

▲ How would you prevent an apple from going brown like this?

▲ Why do onions caramelise?

quickfire

7   What reacts with the enzymes to make bananas go brown?

8   How would you prevent peeled potatoes from discolouring?

Grade boost

Make sure that you can **explain** and give **examples** of enzymic browning, caramelising and gelatinisation.

▼ Why is it important to eat a rainbow of fruit and vegetables?

9   State three qualities you should look for when buying tomatoes.

10   Why do fruit and vegetables spoil more quickly if stored in plastic bags?

Choosing fruit and vegetables

Always choose fruit and vegetables that are 'fresh' looking with a good colour and are not blemished, bruised, wilted or damaged. Eat the produce as soon as possible after purchase and store in either a cool, dry place or the salad drawer in the fridge. Muddy root vegetables will keep for several months in a cold shed or garage. All fruit and vegetables spoil very quickly if stored in plastic packaging.

Do these look like tomatoes you should be buying? ▶

Grade boost

Can you explain the following?

- What happens at each step of the canning process?
- Why are many green, leafy vegetables packaged in MAP?

Processing and preservation

Many fresh fruit and vegetables quickly spoil and decay. They are often processed and preserved to increase the shelf life and give us all-year-round availability. Bacteria, moulds and yeast spoilage are controlled by removing the moisture or oxygen, using heat/cold or altering the pH with sugar, salt or vinegar.

▼ Methods of preservation – make sure you can name them all!

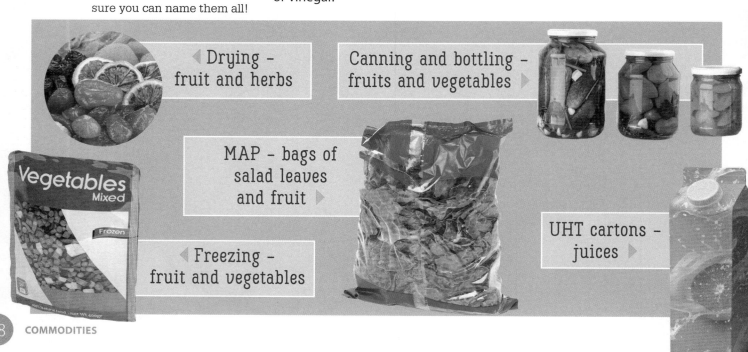

Drying – fruit and herbs ◀

Canning and bottling – fruits and vegetables ▶

MAP – bags of salad leaves and fruit ▶

Freezing – fruit and vegetables ◀

UHT cartons – juices ▶

Preparing fruit and vegetables

- It is best to quickly rinse fruit and vegetables under a cold running tap to clean them.
- DO NOT soak any fruit and vegetables.
- Peel thinly to preserve nutrients found just under the skins.
- Do not prepare green, leafy vegetables too far in advance, to prevent the loss of vital nutrients.

Why do we rinse vegetables rather than soak them?

Thinly peeled and cut carrot strips (batons)

Shredded red cabbage (chiffonade)

Diced (macedoine) peppers

Sliced, fanned strawberry

Julienne carrots

quickfire

11 How would you prepare curly kale or greens for cooking?

quickfire

12 What preparation do strawberries need for a fruit salad?
13 Explain how you would prepare Bramley apples for a pie.

A head of curly kale

Cooking fruit and vegetables

There are a few rules to remember when cooking fruit and vegetables:

1 Vegetables grown **IN** the ground such as potatoes should be submerged in water for cooking and often need a longer cooking time.

2 Vegetables grown **ABOVE** the ground – the stems and leaves – should be cooked in the **minimum** amount of water for the **least** amount of time.

3 Where possible, cook fruit and vegetables in their skins to preserve vitamins and add dietary fibre/NSP.

4 Consider which method of cooking to use, for example steaming preserves many water-soluble vitamins whereas boiled vegetables can have vitamin loss.

5 Serve cooked fruit and vegetables immediately to maintain the vitamins.

6 Never use bicarb when cooking vegetables because the vitamins will be destroyed.

7 Overcooked fruit and vegetables look dull, are very soft and will have lost nutrients.

TOP VEGETABLE COOKING TIPS!

Score or prick skins of potatoes to allow water to escape.

Root vegetables: cover with cold water, bring to boil, simmer until tender.

Green vegetables: plunge into minimum amount of boiling, salted water.

Vegetables such as onions, potatoes and cauliflower florets can be fried in butter or oil.

Can also be stir-fried, usually in a wok.

A mirepoix of vegetables cooked in a stock.

Vegetables such as peppers, courgettes and mushrooms can be brushed with oil and grilled.

Vegetables are placed in perforated steamer trays, where steam builds up to cook them.

Potatoes, squash, peppers and root vegetables can be roasted in a pan containing hot oil. Potatoes and root vegetables are often parboiled before roasting.

Why fruit and vegetables are cooked

1. Softens the **textures** making them easier to eat.

2. Makes them more **digestible**.

3. Improves the **flavours**.

4. Reduces **bulk**.

Seasonality

Foods are in season when they are ripe and ready to harvest or pick. Seasonal fruit and vegetables will be tastier and more nutritious compared to the same foods 'forced' to grow out of season. Fruit and vegetables are widely available and often cheaper when in season.

quickfire

17 Find out when these foods are in season in the UK:
   a) Jersey Royal potatoes
   b) strawberries
   c) leeks
   d) rhubarb
   e) Cox's apples
   f) swedes.

quickfire

14 Name four vegetables that are not usually eaten raw.

15 Give two examples where cooking reduces vegetable bulk.

16 State two vegetables whose flavour is improved by cooking.

▼ A potato field – when are they usually in season in the UK?

Herbs and spices

HERBS ARE THE LEAVES, STEMS AND ROOTS OF PLANTS, USED TO FLAVOUR FOODS:

- BASIL
- BAY
- DILL
- SAGE
- LEMONGRASS
- CORIANDER
- CHIVES
- MINT
- PARSLEY
- ROSEMARY
- HORSERADISH
- TARRAGON
- THYME

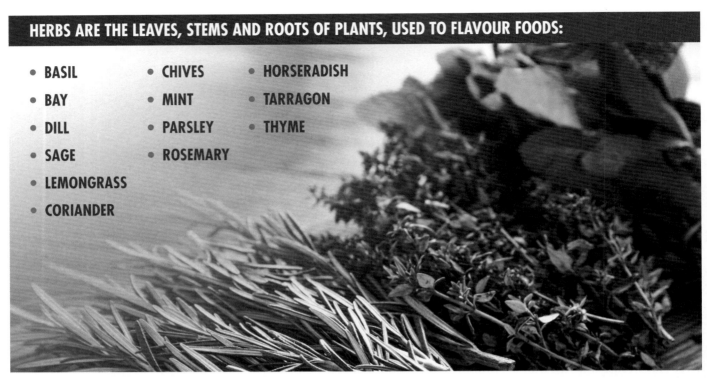

SPICES ARE THE DRIED FLOWERS, SEEDS, LEAVES, BARK AND ROOTS OF AROMATIC PLANTS:

- ALLSPICE
- ANISE-PEPPER
- CARAWAY
- CARDAMOM
- CAYENNE PEPPER
- CHILLI
- CINNAMON
- CLOVES
- CUMIN
- FENUGREEK
- GINGER
- MUSTARD SEED
- PAPRIKA
- PEPPER
- SAFFRON
- SESAME SEED
- TURMERIC

Vegetarian diets

Vegetarians need to eat a wide range of fruit and vegetables to supplement the nutrients they miss from not eating meat and fish.

SOURCE	PROVIDES
Soya beans	Protein
Beans and pulses	Protein
Nuts	Protein
Seeds, walnuts and soya beans	Omega 3
Green, leafy vegetables, dried apricots, figs, sesame and pumpkin seeds, pulses	Iron
Leafy greens	Calcium
Nuts and seeds	Vitamin B2
Nori and kelp	Iodine
Bananas, pulses, nuts and seeds	Potassium

1 Name two fruits and two vegetables rich in vitamin C.

[i] _____

[ii] _____

2 Why is dietary fibre/NSP important in a balanced diet?

_____

_____

3 Identify one 'early' or new crop potato and one main crop potato variety.

_____

_____

4 Describe how to prepare and cook roast potatoes.

_____

_____

5 How should fruit and vegetables be stored?

_____

_____

6 Discuss two ways of preserving fruit and vegetables.

_____

_____

7 Describe the difference between julienne and baton cuts.

_____

_____

8 Discuss the versatility of fruit and vegetables when menu planning.

_____

_____

9 Why should we eat fruit and vegetables when they are in season?

_____

_____

10 How can you tell that green vegetables are fresh?

_____

_____

Sample exam question and answers with commentaries

Q1 Explain how vitamin C can be retained when preparing and cooking fruit and vegetables.

Model answer

When buying fruit and veg make sure that they are fresh because, if they are not, much of the vitamin C will have been lost. Store the fruit and veg in a cool, dark place.

When preparing always use a sharp knife to slice or dice. This minimises cell wall damage, reducing oxidation, which damages vitamin C. Don't prepare fruit and vegetables in advance otherwise vitamin C will be lost.

Never soak vitamin C rich fruit and veg, especially sprouts and cabbage, because the vitamin C will be lost into the water. Steam the vegetables wherever possible because this helps to retain vitamin C or cook the vegetables in the smallest amount of water for the shortest amount of time. Serve them immediately.

Commentary

This answer is excellent. It shows good knowledge of how vitamin C is lost during storage, preparation and cooking. Some 'at risk' vegetables have been identified. There is an understanding of how to minimise vitamin C loss.

Weak answer

Never chop or soak fruit and vegetables because this will cause vitamin C loss. Don't overcook vegetables and use the vegetable water in the gravy.

Commentary

Although two good points have been made this is still classed as a limited answer, so would be awarded lower marks. Compare the detail given in this answer with the model answer.

Q2 How would you cook fresh broccoli?

Model answer

In a steamer or in a saucepan covered with a lid. Use the smallest amount of water and cook for the shortest amount of time until the stems are slightly soft.

Commentary

This answer would achieve top marks. Both boiling and steaming have been identified. Candidate has knowledge that broccoli should not be cooked in large quantities of water.

Weak answer

In a pan of water. Boil until cooked.

Commentary

This is a basic answer because the candidate has only mentioned boiling in water without any further detail.

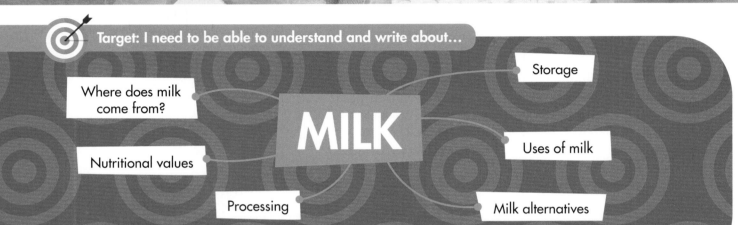

🎯 Target: I need to be able to understand and write about...

Where does milk come from?

Nutritional values

Processing

MILK

Storage

Uses of milk

Milk alternatives

👍 Extra information may be found in the textbook pages 242–246.

▲ Which other animals' milk can we drink?

Grade boost ⌃

Learn these key words and use them in your written work as this will show you understand the question:

Homogenisation

Pasteurisation

Skimming

Sterilising

Ultra-heat treatment (UHT)

Where does milk come from?

Milk is produced by female mammals, usually cows but can be goats or sheep, although only once they have given birth to a calf (kid/lamb). The dairy farmer uses machinery to 'milk' the cows each morning and evening. The milk is stored in chilled vats until it is taken in chilled tankers to the milk processing company.

This milk is referred to as 'raw' milk and cannot be sold to the public unless the farmer has a special licence.

Nutritional values

Milk is a very nutritious food and a particularly good source of **high biological proteins** and calcium. Whole milk contains 4% fat, semi-skimmed milk contains 2% fat and skimmed milk contains 0.1% fat. Milk does **NOT** contain any dietary fibre/NSP.

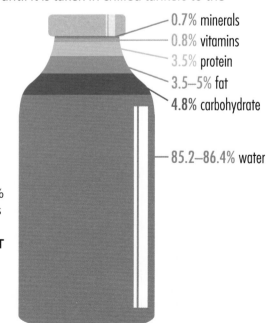

0.7% minerals
0.8% vitamins
3.5% protein
3.5–5% fat
4.8% carbohydrate

85.2–86.4% water

The average composition of cows' milk ▶

Processing milk

Raw milk is heat treated to kill the pathogenic bacteria, thus ensuring it is safe to drink.

Milk processing stages are:

1 PASTEURISATION where milk is heated to 75°C for 25 seconds then rapidly cooled to 5°C.

2 HOMOGENISATION breaks up the fat globules so that they are evenly distributed through the milk, creating an emulsion.

3 SKIMMING the cream (fat) from the milk, which produces semi-skimmed, 1% fat and skimmed milk.

4 STERILISING milk, by placing it into sealed bottles and heating to 110°C–130°C for 30 minutes, meaning it can be stored for months unopened.

5 ULTRA-HEAT TREATING (UHT) where milk is heated to 135°C for 1 second, sealing it into storage packs that can be stored, unopened, for up to six months. Often called 'long-life' milk.

MOST MILK SOLD IN THE UK IS HOMOGENISED

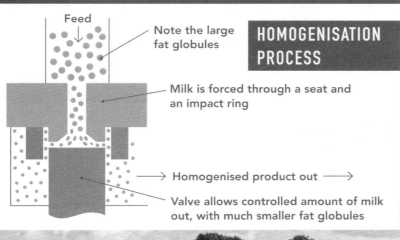

Feed

Note the large fat globules

HOMOGENISATION PROCESS

Milk is forced through a seat and an impact ring

Homogenised product out ⟶

Valve allows controlled amount of milk out, with much smaller fat globules

▼ What does grass make? … Milk!

SECTION 3

quickfire

1 What is the meaning of 'pathogenic'?

2 Name a pathogenic bacterium found in 'raw' milk.

3 Which colour bottle top do the following milks have?
   a) Whole milk
   b) Semi-skimmed milk
   c) Skimmed milk

These milks can then be further processed to produce other milk products, including:

EVAPORATED MILK: 50% of the water is removed from the milk, which is then canned and heat-treated. The texture and flavour change.

CONDENSED MILK: sugar is added to the milk, evaporated, canned and heat-treated to produce a sweet, syrupy milk product.

DRIED MILK: pasteurised milk is sprayed into large, heated chambers where water in the milk evaporates leaving a fine milk powder.

Comparing the fat contents in processed milks

EVAPORATED MILK 4–10% FAT CONTENT

CONDENSED MILK 10% + FAT CONTENT

DRIED MILK 0–3% FAT CONTENT

▲ Do you know what the colour coding on milk bottles represents?

Storage

- Fresh milk **must** be stored in a refrigerator at 5°C. The bottle must have a lid to prevent the milk absorbing any fridge smells such as garlic.

- Keep fresh milk out of sunlight.

- Don't mix old and new milk together.

- Dried milk can be stored in an airtight container and canned milk can be stored in a cupboard indefinitely until opened, when it must be stored in a fridge and used quickly.

quickfire

4 Why should you not mix together old and new milk?

5 Why should fresh milk be kept away from sunlight?

Science

- When milk is heated in a pan it can form a skin on the surface – this shows proteins denaturing. Proteins denature (change) when they are heated, beaten or the pH changes.

▲ Can you explain the changes that take place during denaturing?

Uses of milk

- Drinks, smoothies, on breakfast cereals, milk puddings, white sauces, custard and batter.
- Milk adds nutrients and gives a creamy texture to food. Imagine making custard or a rice pudding with water rather than milk!

Milk type	Recipes that use milk
All fresh, UHT and sterilised milk	In hot drinks, smoothies, white/cheese sauce, custard, panna cotta, batters, rice pudding
Evaporated milk	Pour over desserts, tarte au chocolat, add to coffee
Condensed milk	Fudge, caramel, millionaire shortbread
Dried milk	Add water to the dried milk and use as fresh

How milk can be used ▲

12 Identify different dishes that can be made using each of the following:
    a) skimmed milk
    b) whole milk
    c) dried milk
    d) condensed milk.

Milk alternatives

Milk substitutes can be made from soya beans, almonds, rice, oats and coconuts. These products are used in place of milk by **vegans**, some vegetarians and lactose-intolerant people who can't digest the **lactose** (natural sugar) found in cows' milk. Lactose-intolerance symptoms include painful abdominal bloating, loose, frothy stools and, sometimes, vomiting.

quickfire

6   Why is milk heat treated?
7   Name a bacterium destroyed during pasteurisation
8   Describe how milk is homogenised.
9   Why does the body need protein?
10 Why does the body need calcium?
11 Name a health condition that occurs if not enough calcium is eaten.

Grade boost

Make sure that you can explain how milk is pasteurised and homogenised.

How does the food industry use the fat from skimmed milk?

What factors can make milk 'go off'?

▲ What puddings can you make using condensed milk?

quickfire

13 How many grams of calcium are found in 100ml of each of the following:
    a) soya milk
    b) almond milk
    c) rice milk?
14 What is lactose?
15 Explain why lactose may be a problem for some people to consume.

Target: I need to be able to understand and write about...

Cooking cheese

How milk is processed to make cheese

CHEESE

Nutrients found in cheese

Storage of cheese

Science of cheese production

👍 Extra information may be found in the textbook pages 247–250.

Grade boost

Learn these key words and use them in your written work as this will show you understand the question:

Curds

Mould spores

Whey

How milk is processed to make cheese

HOW IS CHEESE MADE?

 1 A starter culture is added to pasteurised milk to ferment the lactose into lactic acid.

2 The lactic acid is what forms the flavour.

 3 Rennet is then added to coagulate the milk and form curds and whey.

4 The whey is drained.

5 The curds are cut to release more whey.

6 The curds are put under pressure, removing even more whey, to form the cheese.

7 The more whey that is removed the 'harder' the cheese becomes.

8 The cheese is wrapped and left to mature for up to 24 months.

The final cheese made depends on the type of milk used, the makers' recipes, how much whey is removed and additional ingredients added, for example salt, herbs, colourings, fruit and mould.

Categories	Examples
Fresh	cottage cheese, cream cheese, fromage frais, ricotta, mozzarella
Soft	Brie, Camembert, feta
Semi-hard	Edam, St Paulin, Port Salut
Hard	cheddar, Red Leicester, Parmesan, Emmental, Manchego
Blue	Stilton, Danish Blue, Gorgonzola, Roquefort
Processed	cheese slices, cheese strings, spreadable cheese

Cheese is made from fat, protein and water

COTTAGE CHEESE
4g of fat per 100g

FROMAGE FRAIS (PLAIN)
6g of fat per 100g

FETA
16–23g of fat per 100g

MOZZARELLA
22g of fat per 100g

EDAM
25g of fat per 100g

RICOTTA
10g of fat per 100g

PARMESAN
25g of fat per 100g

BRIE
28g of fat per 100g

BLUE STILTON
36g of fat per 100g

CHESHIRE
31g of fat per 100g

CHEDDAR
34g of fat per 100g

MASCARPONE
42g of fat per 100g

quickfire

16 Why does the milk need to coagulate to be able to make cheese?

quickfire

17 What is whey?
18 What are the curds?
19 When would the 'blue' mould spores be added during cheese making?

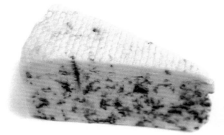

Why does this Danish blue cheese have blue veins in it? ▲

Storage of cheese

Cheese should always be stored in a fridge at 5°C and must be covered or it will dry out. Some cheeses can be frozen but when defrosted the texture may be very crumbly. However, cheese has a better flavour if removed from the fridge about 30 minutes before eating it.

Science of cheese production

- Non-pathogenic **mould spores** are added to cheese to form the blue veins in Stilton and Danish Blue. Fine, stainless steel needles pierce the cheese allowing air to enter so that the blue mould can grow.
- Heated cheese protein denatures, changing the appearance and texture. Think of the difference between a cheese sandwich and a toasted cheese sandwich.
- Heat breaks the protein bonds changing it from a solid to a viscous liquid which hardens when cold.

▲ What happens when rennet is poured into milk and what does this form?

Type	Use
Fresh	Salads, stuffing for chicken breasts and ravioli, cheesecakes
Soft	Baked cheeses, salads, stuffing for chicken breasts
Hard	Cheese sauce, sandwiches, omelettes, in baking, garnishes
Blue	With crackers, stuffing for chicken breasts, sauces

Cooking cheese

- The fat in cheese melts when heated, for example cheese on toast.
- Extreme, dry heat causes cheese protein to become hard or brittle on cooling, for example Parmesan crisps.
- Cheese is used in cooking to add flavour, texture, colour and nutrition.
- It can be used in pastries, breads, sauces, cheesecakes, savoury tarts, as a filling in sandwiches and jacket potatoes, and in salads.
- Cooked cheese is easier to digest than uncooked cheese, because the denatured protein and softened fat make the cheese easier to digest.

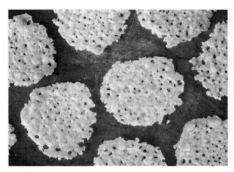

▲ What causes these Parmesan crisps to be so hard?

▲ Why is cheese added to these dauphinoise potatoes?

quickfire

20 Name one dish that can be made using each of the following cheeses:
a) Cheddar
b) Parmesan
c) Stilton
d) Brie
e) Ricotta
f) Gruyere
g) cottage cheese
h) cream cheese.

21 What term is used for the toasted cheese and breadcrumb topping used in cauliflower cheese?

Nutrients found in cheese

Cheese is a good source of:

HBV protein   calcium   fat

Beware!

Many cheeses are roughly one-third saturated fat. A diet high in saturated fat can lead to obesity and vascular/coronary heart disease.

There is **NO** fibre/NSP in cheese.

quickfire

22 What does 'HBV' stand for?
23 Which cheeses contain less than 20% fat?

▼ Do you know why cooked cheese is easier to digest than uncooked cheese?

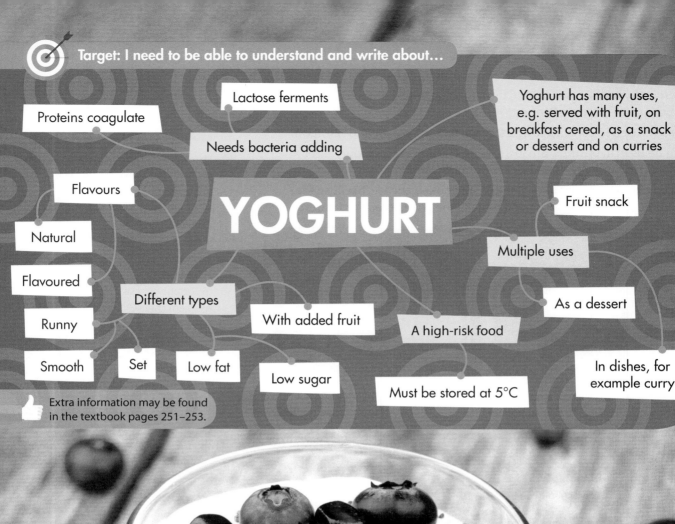

Proteins coagulate

Lactose ferments

Needs bacteria adding

Yoghurt has many uses, e.g. served with fruit, on breakfast cereal, as a snack or dessert and on curries

Flavours

YOGHURT

Natural

Flavoured

Different types

Fruit snack

Multiple uses

Runny

With added fruit

A high-risk food

As a dessert

Smooth   Set   Low fat

Low sugar

Must be stored at 5°C

In dishes, for example curry

👍 Extra information may be found in the textbook pages 251–253.

How is yoghurt made?

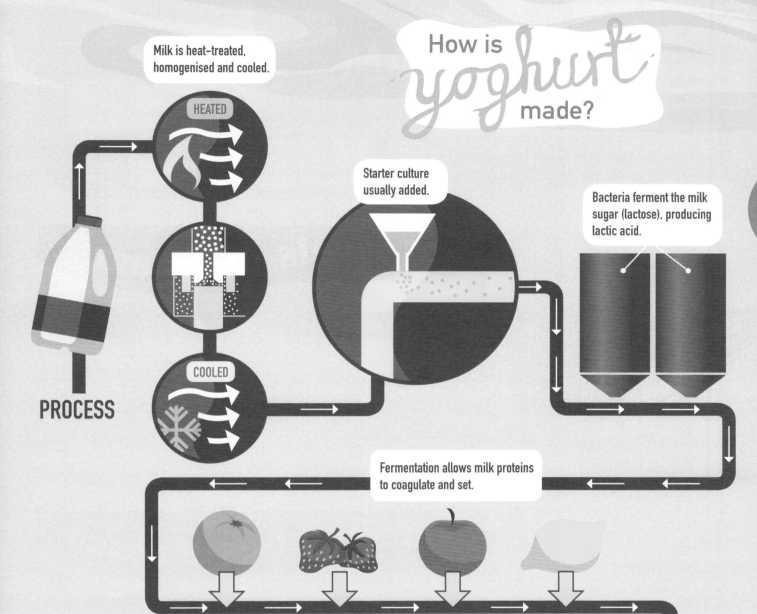

Milk is heat-treated, homogenised and cooled.

HEATED

Starter culture usually added.

Bacteria ferment the milk sugar (lactose), producing lactic acid.

COOLED

PROCESS

Fermentation allows milk proteins to coagulate and set.

Sugar, sweetener, fruit or fruit flavouring added.

Yoghurt is packaged and chilled.

Yoghurt is made from different types of milk, including skimmed, semi-skimmed, whole, evaporated or powdered forms.

SECTION 3

Target: I need to be able to understand and write about...

CREAM

Cream is the fat that has been separated from milk

Cream adds a creamy texture to food as well as a rich flavour

All cream is pasteurised to destroy any harmful bacteria

Always store cream at 5°C with the lid firmly attached

UHT cream can be stored, unopened, in a cupboard

Cream has high fat levels ranging from 18% per 100g to 55+% per 100g

Extra information may be found in the textbook pages 254–257.

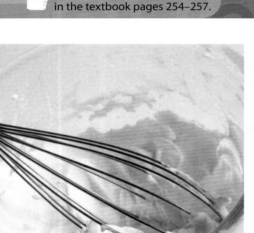

Can you explain what happens to the cream during whisking? ▲

Fat levels in cream

TYPE OF CREAM	FAT %/100G
Single	18%
Crème fraîche	30%
Whipping	35%
Double	48%
Clotted	55–64%

quickfire

24 State two uses for each of the following types of cream:
   a) single
   b) crème fraîche
   c) whipping
   d) double
   e) clotted.

Different uses of cream

TYPE OF CREAM	USES
Single	Pouring over desserts or in coffee. Cannot be whisked.
Whipping	Pouring or whisked for piping onto cakes and desserts.
Double	Whisked into and piped onto desserts. Can be used for pouring.
Clotted	Formed into quenelles on scones and desserts. It must not be stirred or beaten.

How is CREAM produced?

The production process involves separation of the fat from the milk which is done through centrifugation. Centrifugation involves spinning the milk at high speed; the force of this process causes the milk-fat globules to separate from the watery liquid to produce **single cream**. This process is continued to produce **double cream**. All cream is then pasteurised to destroy any harmful bacteria.

Clotted cream

- Fresh cows' milk is placed in a shallow pan and left for 6–14 hours
- Cream floats to the surface of the milk.
- This mixture is then heated over a water bath at a temperature of 80–90°C for 40–50 minutes.
- Cooled for 24 hours and 'clots' of cream with a firm yellow crust are formed. This cream is removed, 'potted' up and sold as clotted cream.
- The liquid left over is skimmed milk.
- Clotted cream has a rich, buttery flavour, and thick, creamy consistency.

Whipping cream

- Made by mixing cream with air.
- Volume doubles.
- Air bubbles are captured in fat droplets.

Long-life cream

- Produced from UHT milk.
- High temperatures during UHT processing give a slightly caramelised flavour.
- Unopened cream can be stored at ambient temperatures for several months.
- Once opened must be stored in a refrigerator.

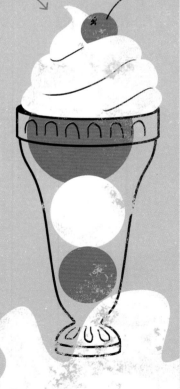

Soured cream

- Cream with a bacterial culture added.
- Produces lactic acid.
- This sours and thickens the product.

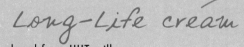

Crème fraîche

- Made by adding bacterial culture to cream.
- A soured product.

1 Give two reasons why milk is necessary in a child's diet.

[i] _____

_____

[ii] _____

_____

2 Some people cannot digest milk. What is this condition called?

_____

3 Describe how milk should be safely stored.

_____

_____

_____

4 Name two nutrients, other than calcium, found in whole milk.

[i] _____

[ii] _____

5 Name two types of milk that do not need to be stored in the fridge.

[i] _____

[ii] _____

6 Describe the processes that milk goes through at a commercial dairy.

_____

_____

_____

_____

7 State the pathogenic bacterium for which all cow herds are tested.

_____

8 Give one reason why yoghurt should be stored in a fridge.

_____

_____

_____

9 Identify two soft cheeses, two hard cheeses and two blue cheeses.

[i] _____

[ii] _____

[iii] _____

[iv] _____

[v] _____

[vi] _____

10 How can cheese be made more digestible?

_____

_____

_____

_____

11 Describe what happens to cheese on heating.

_____

_____

_____

_____

Sample exam question and answers with commentaries

Q1 Discuss the choice and use of dairy products in food preparation and cooking.

Model answer

Dairy foods include milk, cheese, yoghurt, cream and butter, with milk, cheese and yoghurt supplying good levels of protein and calcium.

Nearly all milk in the UK is pasteurised to kill harmful bacteria before turning it into yoghurt, cheese, cream and butter. The milk is heated to 75°C for 25 seconds and then rapidly cooled to 5°C. All dairy foods must be stored in a fridge to prevent spoilage.

Milk is used for drinks, smoothies, milk puddings and sauces. It adds nutrients and a creaminess to the dishes.

Yoghurt comes in several forms - set, runny, flavoured and low fat. Yoghurt can be eaten as a snack, with breakfast cereal and fruit, in salad dressings, as toppings on curry and in desserts, and as a healthy alternative to cream.

Cheese is made by 'setting' the milk into solids and removing the whey. This is done using rennet. Cheese is rich in protein and calcium but it also has a high fat content. There are many different varieties of cheese such as cheddar, Brie, Wensleydale, Parmesan and ricotta. When cooking, the correct cheese must be chosen, e.g. to have a stringy melted cheese topping on a pizza use a soft creamy cheese such as mozzarella, whereas to get the au gratin topping on a dish cheddar is a better option because mozzarella or Parmesan wouldn't melt as easily. Some creamy cheeses such as mascarpone cheese can be used in uncooked desserts. Cheese flavours and adds nutrients to foods.

Cream is the fat from milk and should be used sparingly. Single cream doesn't hold air so is used to pour on fruit and desserts, whereas double cream can be whisked making it light and airy. This can be piped onto gateaux and desserts.

Butter is made from the milk cream and is very high in fat, but when used in cooking adds a rich flavour and colour to food. It is spread onto bread, and used in cake, biscuit and pastry making.

Commentary

This is an excellent answer that would access higher band marks. It covers different types of dairy foods giving clear examples of uses and there is justification of the foods' use. The answer is balanced in that both food prep and cooking are referenced.

SECTION 3

Weaker answer

Dairy products are used a lot in cooking. Milk in smoothies and milkshakes, cheese in sandwiches or on toast and yoghurt for breakfast. That's because dairy foods are good for you. They must be kept in a fridge or they will go off. Some people are allergic to milk.

Commentary

This would get low level marks because although several points have been made there are no supporting explanations. The answer does not illustrate a depth of knowledge of dairy foods. This can be seen quite easily when comparing this answer with the model answer.

MEAT, POULTRY, FISH AND EGGS

 Target: I need to be able to understand and write about...

Nutritional values

Processing

MEAT, POULTRY AND FISH

What meat is and the different types

Buying

Pointers for buying

Science

Extra information may be found in the textbook pages 262–293.

Storage, cooking and uses

Meat, poultry, offal, game and fish

Meat refers to the muscle and flesh from farmed animals such as cows, lambs and pigs, and 'poultry' birds including chickens, ducks and turkeys.

There are different types of chicken:

SPRING CHICKEN

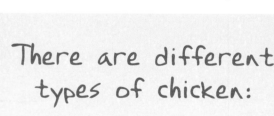

POUSSIN

CAPON

BOILING FOWL

TYPES OF POULTRY

TURKEY

DUCK

GUINEA FOWL

GOOSE

QUAIL

WOOD PIGEON

PHEASANT

OSTRICH

111

TYPES OF OFFAL

Offal is the edible internal organs, for example liver, heart and kidney.

Liver

FACTS
An important component of the Scottish national dish, haggis, and often used in Italian cooking, where it is valued for its spongy texture.

Liver is an excellent source of iron and Vitamin A.

Ox liver

Lamb's liver

Kidney

FACTS
Kidneys are particularly popular as food in European nations such as England, France, Spain and Sweden.

Heart

FACTS
Can be very chewy in texture.

Heart meat is high in protein, iron, selenium, phosphorus and zinc.

Tail

FACTS
The bony tails of the ox and pig have rich meat on them. The fatty ones from fat-tailed sheep have no bone and are highly valued in the Middle East.

Tongue

FACTS
Calfs' and lambs' tongues need to be soaked then boiled to rid them of the blood and then peeled.

Tripe

FACTS
Tripe is stomach lining and it resembles a honeycomb.

Sweetbread

FACTS
Obtained from calves and lambs. It is a highly prized ingredient in French cooking. Sweetbreads are an organ meat from the thymus gland and pancreas.

Game meat comes from 'wild' animals and birds such as rabbit, pheasant, pigeon and deer (venison).

Fish is taken from seas and rivers. Fish is classified into three types: white fish, oily fish and shellfish.

Processing

The farming and slaughtering of animals for food is controlled by very strict regulations so that animals:

1. do not experience cruelty
2. have shelter
3. are fed well
4. have clean water to drink
5. are free from injury/disease.

For public safety, all meat and meat products must be traceable throughout the food chain to show that all regulations have been met.

Most animals are stunned before slaughter, then skinned before the carcass is opened up and the internal organs removed. The carcass is then 'hung' in a cold room for several hours and up to three weeks, allowing meat enzymes to develop flavour and soften the texture before the meat is butchered into smaller cuts.

Grade boost

Learn these key words and use them in your written work as this will show you understand the question:

Maillard reaction

Myoglobin

quickfire

1 Name:
a) one red meat
b) two poultry meats
c) two oily fish
d) two white fish
e) two shellfish.

▼ Can you recall the cuts of meat on these animals?

SECTION 3

Smaller fish are killed and gutted (the internal organs are removed) before sale, whereas larger fish are cut into fillets, cutlets and steaks, e.g. salmon, tuna and cod. Fresh fish goes off quickly so must be used within a few days of catch or frozen to increase the shelf life.

quickfire

2 State three cuts of beef and three cuts of pork.
3 Name three 'small' types of fish.

Common cuts of fish – are they from large fish or small fish? ▶

Fillet

Steak

Cutlet

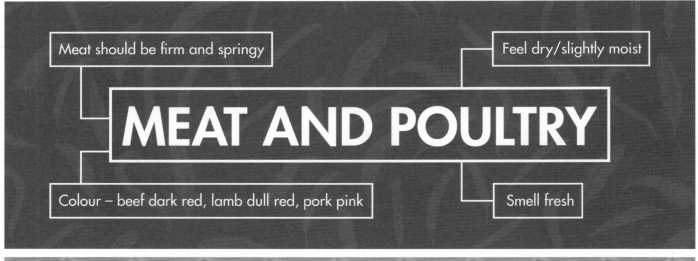

MEAT AND POULTRY

- Meat should be firm and springy
- Feel dry/slightly moist
- Colour – beef dark red, lamb dull red, pork pink
- Smell fresh

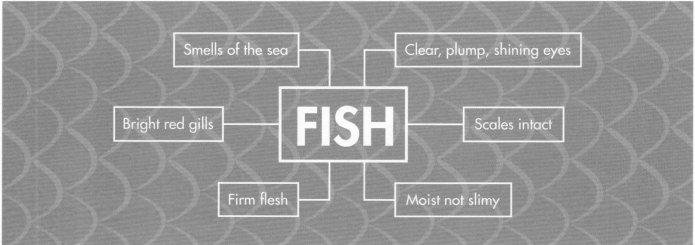

FISH

- Smells of the sea
- Clear, plump, shining eyes
- Bright red gills
- Scales intact
- Firm flesh
- Moist not slimy

Grade boost

Describe the physical differences between red meat and offal.

Why is the flesh of oily fish coloured but the flesh of white fish white?

COMMON BACTERIA INFECTING HUMANS

Salmonella

Campylobacter

Escherichia coli

Staphylococcus aureus

Storing meat, poultry and fish

Meat, poultry and fish:

- Should be bought from a reputable supplier.
- Should be stored in a leak-proof container
- Must be stored at 5°C on the bottom shelf of a fridge.
- Raw meat, poultry and fish must be stored on a shelf below cooked meat, poultry and fish.
- Must be used as soon as possible or frozen to use later.
- Fish and offal should be used the same day as purchase because they 'go off' very quickly.

Raw meat, poultry and fish can cause food poisoning due to incorrect storage, cross-contamination from food handlers not washing their hands and equipment after preparation, and the meat, poultry and fish not being cooked thoroughly.

All raw meat, poultry and fish carry pathogenic bacteria such as Salmonella, Campylobacter and E. coli, with raw chicken being the main source for campylobacter contamination.

Cooking meat, poultry and fish

Fish can be poached, steamed, grilled, fried, baked or microwaved. It is very tender and cooks quickly but is easily overcooked, which hardens the fish 'meat'.

4 Describe how you would store the following:
   a) fresh trout
   b) raw chicken pieces
   c) prawn cocktail.

5 Raw chicken is a source of which pathogenic bacteria?

▼ What type of heat transfer is at work in each of these processes?

boiling

frying

steaming

stewing

spit roasting

poaching

barbeque

roasting

pot roasting

grilling

chargrill

SECTION 3

quickfire

6   a) What does 'denaturing protein' mean?
    b) Give two examples of denatured protein food.
7   What is the benefit of the Maillard reaction to some cuts of meat?

 Maillard reaction – think steak!

quickfire

8   Can you name two amino acids?
9   What is understood by the term 'lean meat'?
10   Why does white fish lack omega 3?
11   How can eating too much saturated fat affect the body?

Grade boost

Learn a range of dishes that can be made from different cuts of beef, pork, lamb and chicken. This will enable you to give examples in the extended questions.

Science

Oxygen – turns the red **myoglobin** in meat brown, while chicken and fish discolour and become unpleasant to smell.

Heat and **acid** – both denature (unravel) and coagulate (set or harden) the proteins in meat, poultry and fish. These changes cannot be reversed. Cooking softens the connective tissue but if the proteins are overcooked they become hard, tough and dry. Acid, as in lemon juice and tomatoes, also softens meat connective tissue. Lime juice 'cooks' raw fish.

Maillard reaction – when meat is cooked on a hot, dry pan the surface will brown and different flavour compounds are formed. The browning is due to the reaction between the meat's natural sugars and proteins. Flavour changes are due to the heat on the natural sugars giving the distinctive roasted meat flavour.

Enzymes – animal carcasses are stored for up to 28 days to allow the natural enzymes in the meat to soften muscle fibres and develop the meat flavour.

Nutritive values

Note: There is **NO** fibre/NSP in any animal product.

The **main** nutrients associated with meat, poultry and fish are shown in the table below.

NUTRIENT	CATEGORY	SOURCE
Protein	High biological value (HBV) protein	All meat, poultry, fish and shellfish
Fat	Saturated fat Unsaturated fat Omega 3	All meat and poultry All meat, poultry and oily fish Oily fish
Iron	Mineral	Red meat, liver
Vitamins A and D B group vitamins	Vitamins	Oily fish and meat Red meat, especially B12

The fat of white fish is found in the liver and is processed into fish liver oils, for example cod liver oil.

Uses

Meat, poultry and fish form the basis of most main meals because they can all be cooked in various ways to add variety to the diet.

Meat – make sure the correct cut of meat is used for the dish to be made. Tough cuts need long, slow, moist cooking, whereas tender cuts cook very quickly.

To tenderise tough cuts of meat add an acidic ingredient, such as tomatoes or wine, to the marinade or casserole. The acid 'breaks down' the tougher meat collagen 'softening' it.

Shin of beef	Tough cut 2 hours	Stews and casseroles
Sirloin steak	Tender cut 2–5 minutes	Dry-pan fried
Belly pork	Tough cut 1–2 hours	Slow cooked
Chicken breast	Tender cut 15+ minutes	Roasted, fried
Chicken leg/thigh	Tough cut 45+ minutes	Slow roast, casserole

Fish readily absorbs strong flavours such as chilli and lime, so these make good marinades for it.

Nutrition value of 100g of fish					
	Energy (kcal)	Protein (g)	Fat (g)	Calcium (mg)	Vitamin A (µg)	Vitamin D (µg)
Cod, grilled	85	21	1.3	10	2	1
Mackerel, grilled	239	21	17.3	12	48	8.8
Salmon, grilled	215	24	13	25	16	7.1
Salmon, canned	153	24	6.6	91	31	9.2

quickfire

12 What can you use to help tenderise meat?

▲ Do you know how meat is cured? Research it in the textbook or on the internet.

▲ Roasted meat. What joint could this be?

▲ Braised meat. What cut is this likely to be?

quickfire

13 Name three tough cuts of beef and lamb.
14 State two tender cuts of beef and lamb.
15 Name three meat dishes that use tough cuts.

SECTION 3

▲ Grilled, poached and shallow fried fish. Can you suggest a dish using each of these methods?

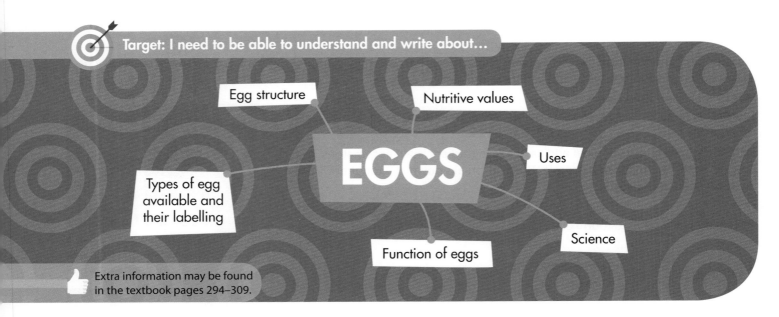

Target: I need to be able to understand and write about...

Egg structure

Nutritive values

EGGS

Types of egg available and their labelling

Uses

Function of eggs

Science

Extra information may be found in the textbook pages 294–309.

Extra information may be found in the textbook pages 294–309.

Types and labelling of eggs

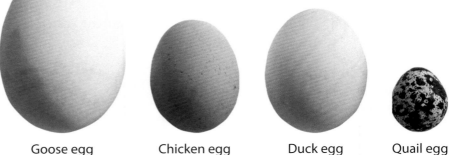

| Goose egg | Chicken egg | Duck egg | Quail egg |

Eggs are produced by all female birds. However, in the UK we eat mainly chickens' eggs, although goose, duck and quail eggs are available. Eggs are classified according to how the chickens are reared. The cheapest eggs available are usually 'battery' reared. Eggs can also be **barn, free-range** or **organic**. The information printed on all egg shells shows the country of origin, the code for the farm and the method used for egg production, the lion/dragon mark and a 'best before' date.

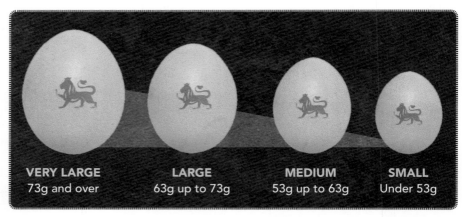

| **VERY LARGE** 73g and over | **LARGE** 63g up to 73g | **MEDIUM** 53g up to 63g | **SMALL** Under 53g |

▲ Welsh eggs have a dragon mark on their shells.

QUICKFIRE

16 Do you know any other birds' eggs that are eaten in other countries? Research this on the internet if you need to.

Grade boost

Learn these key words and use them in your written work as this will show you understand the question:

Albumen

Barn eggs

Campylobacter

Free range

Organic

Salmonella

Syneresis

QUICKFIRE

17 Can you describe the different egg producing methods?

18 What does the lion/dragon mark mean?

Structure of an egg

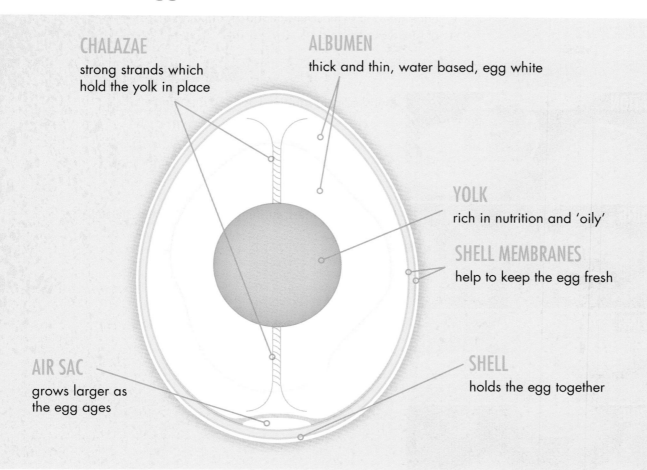

CHALAZAE
strong strands which
hold the yolk in place

ALBUMEN
thick and thin, water based, egg white

YOLK
rich in nutrition and 'oily'

SHELL MEMBRANES
help to keep the egg fresh

AIR SAC
grows larger as
the egg ages

SHELL
holds the egg together

Nutritive values

- Eggs contain nearly all the nutrients we regularly need.
- They are a good source of HBV protein and omega 3.
- Eggs are rich in vitamins A, D, E, riboflavin (B2) and B1, along with traces of other vitamins and minerals.
- There is **NO** vitamin C or fibre/NSP in eggs.
- Eggs are a cheap source of protein food compared to meat and fish.
- There is no nutritional difference between brown and white shelled eggs – different breeds produce different-coloured shells.

Quickfire

19 Explain each part of the egg structure.

Grade boost

Name the protein in egg white.

Typical values	Per medium size egg	Per 100g
Energy	277kJ 66kcal	547kJ 131kcal
Fat	4.6g	9.0g
of which saturates	1.3g	2.5g
monounsaturates	1.7g	3.4g
polyunsaturates	0.7g	1.4g
Carbohydrate of which sugars	Trace	Trace
Protein	6.4g	12.6g
Salt	0.2g	0.4g

Functions of eggs

Eggs are used extensively in food production because they have a range of functions.

FUNCTION	EXAMPLES
AERATION	Mousses, cold soufflés, sponges, meringues
BINDING	Fish cakes, burgers, stuffing, meatloaf, rissoles, falafel
COATING	Scotch eggs, fish cakes, rissoles, fish in batter
GLAZING	Savoury pastry dishes, bread, scones
EMULSIFYING	Mayonnaise, aioli, creaming mixture for cakes
THICKENING	Sauce, custards, soups
ENRICHING	Sauces, custards, mashed potato, milk puddings, pasta dishes
GARNISH	Salads

Storage of eggs

There are no strict rules for storing eggs. They can be left at room temperature or in a fridge for up to three weeks. They should be stored 'point' end down and not next to strong smelling foods like garlic and fish because these smells will be absorbed, tainting the egg flavour. Once the egg is out of the shell it must be covered, stored in the fridge and used quickly. As eggs age the **albumen** loses water and 'plumpness', becoming very runny and thin. Eggs have a neutral smell and should not be used if they have developed a smell. To test for egg freshness gently drop it into a jug of water. If it sinks it is fresh, if it floats it is stale. It floats due to the amount of air inside the egg.

Science of eggs

Heat denatures egg protein, with egg albumen coagulating at 60°C, changing from a clear liquid to a white solid, and the egg yolk thickening from 65°C–70°C. This helps to set custards, cakes and quiches. Adding sugar to the egg mixture increases the coagulation temperature. An over-heated egg mixture causes **syneresis** or curdling, where the liquid oozes out of the set mixture.

Whisked eggs can hold a large volume of air, forming a foam to make 'airy' meringues and mousses. A drop of lemon juice (acid) added to egg white makes the meringue slightly mallowy, whereas adding a pinch of salt decreases the pH making it more stable and enhances the meringue flavour.

Uses of eggs

Eggs are foods in their own right, such as boiled eggs and omelettes, or are added to ingredients forming dishes such as Swiss roll, mayonnaise, custard and falafels. Many recipes include eggs to make the dish 'work'.

How many dishes can you name that use hard-boiled eggs?

How is a quiche filling set?

What forms the mayonnaise emulsion?

What is the light, airy texture of a mousse reliant on?

SECTION 3

quickfire

21 State the coagulation temperature for:
a) albumen
b) egg yolk coagulate.

quickfire

22 Name two dishes that illustrate eggs' function as a:
a) food
b) aerator
c) emulsifier
d) glaze
e) binding
f) setting agent
g) coating
h) thickener
i) enricher
j) garnish.

Meat, poultry and fish

1 State two types of red meat and two types of poultry eaten in the UK.

   [i] _____

   [ii] _____

2 Name two **micronutrients** found in red meat.

   [i] _____

   [ii] _____

3 State why vitamin B12, found in red meat, is vital for good health.

   _____

   _____

   _____

   _____

4 Discuss why we should eat lean meat.

   _____

   _____

   _____

   _____

5 State three nutrients, other than omega 3, found in oily fish.

   [i] _____

   [ii] _____

   [iii] _____

6 Fresh fish has a very short shelf life. Describe two ways that fish can be preserved.

   [i] _____

   _____

   _____

   [ii] _____

   _____

   _____

Sample exam questions and answers with commentaries

Q1 Discuss the following points to be considered when preparing and cooking meat:
[i] nutritional value   [ii] choices available   [iii] uses.

Model answer

Nutritional values - meat is eaten because it contains HBV protein, with all the essential amino acids needed for growth and repair of the body. Red meat, such as beef, is a good source of iron, needed for haemoglobin, which transports oxygen around the body. Meat contains saturated fat that can cause heart disease. There is no dietary fibre in meat.

Choices available - we eat mainly beef, chicken, lamb and pork although other meats are available such as venison, rabbit, turkey and pheasant. Tough cuts of meat such as stewing steak, belly pork and chicken legs need long, slow cooking to soften the tough strands of muscle. Tender cuts such as sirloin steak, chicken breast and lamb chops come from muscle that hasn't been worked hard. These cook quickly so don't need tenderising. Products such as sausages and burgers are made from minced meats.

Uses - small pieces of meat such as steak and burgers cook quickly when dry fried or grilled. Large joints of meat such as chicken, and shoulder of lamb need longer, slower cooking to soften the muscle fibres. Pieces of meat can be used in stews such as beef bourgignon, stir fries and pies. It is important to use the correct cut of meat for the chosen dish.

Commentary

This has been answered using three headings. Doing this helps to keep a focus on each topic. The answers given show good knowledge and understanding of 'meat'. A range of good examples support the statements made. This response would access high band marks.

Weaker answer

Chicken is the most popular meat to eat but you can eat beef and lamb too. It is very good for us because of the protein. But meat has lots of fat and that is bad for us. You can make stews, roasts and burgers from meat.

Commentary

This is a low band response due to a lack of detailed knowledge. Nutrition – only one reference to protein. Three uses have been identified with no explanation. Compare this answer with the model answer.

Q2 Explain why our diets should include oily fish.

Model answer

Oily fish adds variety to the diet and is very quick and easy to cook. It can be pan fried or grilled easily. It is a really good source of protein for people recovering from illness and surgery because it is easy to digest. Oily fish, like mackerel and sardines, is good brain food because it aids our concentration. It also helps to reduce the risk of heart disease and strokes due to omegas 3 and 6 - good fats found in oily fish - as well as the mono- and polyunsaturated fats, which are also 'good fats'.

Commentary

This is a good high band answer. There is reference to protein, ease of digestion, oily fish and their fats. This shows some good knowledge and understanding.

Weaker answer

Fish is good for us and we should eat it three times a week, like cod or tuna. It has protein. Some vegetarians eat fish.

Commentary

This is a very limited answer that would access low band marks. The student should think – why eat fish three times a week? Are there any other nutrients in it? The last statement is irrelevant to the question.

EXAM QUESTIONS

Eggs

1 Name three types of egg, other than chicken eggs, that can be used in cooking.

[i] _____

[ii] _____

[iii] _____

2 What is the name of the protein in egg white?

_____

_____

_____

_____

_____

3 State the two macronutrients found in eggs.

[i] _____

[ii] _____

4 Identify five functions of eggs.

[i] _____

[ii] _____

[iii] _____

[iv] _____

[v] _____

5 Give three ways of cooking eggs.

[i] _____

[ii] _____

[iii] _____

6 Describe what happens when egg white is whisked.

_____

_____

_____

_____

_____

_____

_____

_____

_____

_____

_____

7 What can stop an egg white from foaming?

_____

_____

_____

_____

8 State why eggs are used when making:

a) goujons _____

_____

b) mayonnaise _____

_____

_____

_____

c) Cornish pasties _____

_____

_____

Sample exam question and answers with commentaries

Q1 Eggs are widely used when making food.

Explain the nutritional values of eggs, choice of eggs and how they are used.

Model answer

Nutritional values

Eggs are rich in high biological protein needed for growth and repair and the yolk contains fat for hormone production and body warmth. A medium-sized egg has about 75-90kcals, which isn't too high if you are weight-watching. There is no fibre in eggs.

Choices

Most eggs are from chickens but it is possible to buy goose, duck and quail eggs. A duck egg equals two or three chicken eggs and a quail egg is about half a chicken egg. Eggs aren't expensive for protein food but very cheap eggs probably come from caged battery farms. Free range chickens roam outdoors but the eggs are dearer. Eggs produced organically are covered by very strict Soil Association rules.

Uses

Eggs are used in cooking because when heated to 65°C proteins denature and harden causing the mixture to thicken or set, e.g. custard and quiche, but will shrink and lose water forming syneresis if overcooked. They hold lots of air when whisked, which is needed for meringues and mousses. If sugar or a pinch of salt is added the egg white foam becomes more stable but if any fat or oil gets into egg white it will never be able to hold air. Egg yolk helps emulsify oil and water so it is used to make mayonnaise from oil and vinegar. Eggs are used for food, e.g. poached egg on toast. They can be glazed onto pastry for a golden shine on pies.

Commentary

The response has been set out in a way that each part of the question has been clearly answered: nutritional values, choices and uses. This helps maintain the focus of the question. It is clear that the student has good knowledge and understanding for each part of the question. This answer would have accessed high marks.

Weaker answer

Eggs are good for you because they help you to grow. They are used to make custard, quiche or in a breakfast fry-up. They go rubbery in cooking. Some vegetarians don't eat eggs because they are from animals. Eggs have egg white and yolk, the yellow bit.

Commentary

It is easy to see the difference between this answer and the model answer. Each statement needs justifying and it is important to use correct subject vocabulary, for example eggs set or coagulate rather than 'go rubbery'. There is no mention of nutrients and protein in particular.

This answer would access low band marks.

SECTION 3

BEANS, NUTS, SEEDS, SOYA, TOFU AND MYCOPROTEIN

 Target: I need to be able to understand and write about...

BEANS, NUTS, SEEDS, SOYA, TOFU AND MYCOPROTEIN

- Types available
- Processing
- Allergens
- Uses
- Nutritional values

👍 Extra information may be found in the textbook pages 318–331.

Types available

Pulses are edible seeds that grow in a pod, which include all types of beans, lentils and peas. They belong to the **legume** family.

Nuts are hard-shelled fruits, except for peanuts, which are legumes.
Seeds, such as sunflower seeds, pumpkin seeds and sesame seeds, are the embryos of plants.

▼ Can you identify these seeds?

Grade boost

Learn this key word and use it in your written work as this will show you understand the question:
Legume

quickfire

1 Name two beans, lentils, peas and nuts.

Grade boost

Learn the terms 'pulse' and 'legume' and what they mean.

Processing

Pulses, nuts and seeds require little processing to be used as ingredients.

Beans, peas, lentils (pulses)

These are either dried or canned.

Dried beans and peas need to be soaked before use.

Dried kidney beans must be soaked for 12 hours and then **boiled** for at least ten minutes to destroy the natural toxin, lectin.

Canned pulses have been both soaked and cooked.

Nuts

Nuts can be simply shelled and eaten 'raw'.

Nuts can be pressed to extract the oil, such as walnut and almond oils.

Seeds

Seeds can be cleaned, ground and pressed to extract the oil, which is then filtered and refined to get the correct colour and flavour. Examples are sunflower and sesame oils.

Nutritional values

Pulses are a cheap, low fat, source of low biological protein and therefore non-meat eaters must eat a range of them to get all the amino acids the body needs. Pulses contain starch, dietary fibre/NSP and iron.

Nuts contain low biological value protein, dietary fibre/NSP and essential fatty acids and, in some nuts, vitamin E and calcium. They are good for a non-meat eater's diet but if eaten to excess provide the body with too much fat. Salted nuts should be eaten sparingly due to the high levels of salt. Some people develop an allergy to nuts, which can be life threatening.

quickfire

2 Write one sentence for each about three different pulses.

3 Why must dried kidney beans be soaked for a long time and then boiled for at least ten minutes before using?

Seeds are an excellent source of protein and micro-nutrients such as the B group vitamins, calcium and zinc. Sunflower seeds are high in vitamin E. Sunflower oil should be used sparingly because of the fat levels.

quickfire

4 State three dishes that include two or more pulses.

5 Why is it good to snack on pumpkin seeds rather than sweets?

6 Which amino acid is lacking in nuts?

Grade boost

Why does the body need the amino acid lacking in nuts?

▲ Almond

▲ Brazil

▲ Cashew

▲ Pecan

▲ Pistachio

▲ Hazelnut

▲ Walnut

▲ Macadamia

Uses

PULSES

NUTS

SEEDS

Alternative proteins and their uses

Alternative 'novel protein' foods are used by vegans and vegetarians to replace meat in the diet. It has been calculated that using the same amount of land to grow vegetable protein as it takes to rear one beef cattle produces greater quantities of food, so growing vegetable protein foods is essential for feeding the growing populations.

Popular alternative proteins are made from soya beans and mycoproteins.

Tofu

Tofu is made from soya bean curd and used in many meat – and dairy free – products.

Textured vegetable protein

Textured vegetable protein (TVP) is made from soya flour and used in vegetarian ready-made meals. It is a cheap ingredient used to bulk out meat products in order to reduce manufacturing costs.

Quorn

Quorn is a fermented fungus called mycoprotein. It is processed into meat styled products such as 'chicken' fillets, burgers and sausages. Some Quorn products use milk or eggs during processing so are not suitable for vegans.

Nutritional values

Soya beans, tofu and TVP are excellent sources of high biological protein (HBV), calcium and iron, and are low in fat. Quorn is an excellent source of HBV and dietary fibre/NSP, and is low in fat and sodium. Nutritionally, these foods are excellent alternatives to meat.

quickfire

7 Name three dishes that can be made using tofu.
8 What does TVP stand for?
9 What does HBV stand for?
10 What are the health benefits of using alternative proteins in place of meat?

Grade boost

What does HBV stand for?

EXAM QUESTIONS

1   State two sources of vegetable protein.

[i] _____

[ii] _____

2   What is meant by LBV?

_____

_____

_____

_____

_____

_____

3   Which is the only HBV bean?

_____

4   What is meant by complementary proteins?

_____

_____

_____

_____

5   Give examples of different complementary protein meals.

_____

_____

_____

_____

6   Describe the different types of vegetarians.

_____

_____

_____

_____

_____

Sample exam question and answers with commentaries

Q1 Discuss how vegans can get enough protein in their diets

Model answer

Vegans do not eat any animal foods or by-products such as bees' honey. For most people protein is easily obtained from meat, milk, cheese, fish and eggs, none of which vegans can eat. These proteins are called high biological value proteins because they have all the essential amino acids. Vegans rely on low biological value protein plants and grains for the important nutrients, especially protein. Good sources of protein come from soya, tofu, TVP and Quorn products because these are HBV proteins and contain all the essential amino acids needed for growth, cell maintenance and repair. However, vegans also eat LBV protein ingredients such as flour, nuts, seeds and pulses. It is important that vegans mix and match these ingredients to ensure they consume the full range of amino acid proteins. Vegans should have variety in their diet; if they rely on just a few ingredients they may become deficient is some vital amino acids that the body cannot make.

Soya, TVP and tofu meat substitutes can be used to make vegetable lasagne, chilli, casseroles and stews and the nutritional content of these will be similar to their meat versions.

Commentary

The knowledge and understanding of vegan requirements is clearly shown in this answer, which would access the higher level marks. To make this a brilliant answer the student could have named one LBV protein food and identified which amino acid it lacked.

Weaker answer

Animal protein is the best and vegetable protein isn't as good. Protein is important to us. So vegans need to eat lots of vegetable protein such as flour and beans. Some beans are better than others. To make it easier they can buy ready-made veggie dishes like vegetable curry or veggie burgers.

Commentary

This is a weak, low band mark, answer. It is clear the student knows there is a difference between animal and vegetable protein and that protein is vital for health. However, no reasons or justifications have been given.

Q2 Explain the nutritional values, choices and uses of pulses in the diet.

Model answer

Pulses include peas, beans and lentils and are used in vegetarian and vegan diets because they are good sources of non-animal protein. Most pulses are classed as LBV but soya beans and soya products contain all the essential amino acids so are classed as HBV proteins. Pulses are low in fat and contain good levels of dietary fibre/NSP.

Pulses are purchased in a dried form, which will need rehydrating, or canned where they have been soaked and cooked.

Pulses are used in stews, casseroles, bean salads, beans on toast, chickpeas into hummus, lentils into soup or lentil bake.

Commentary

This answer is very good and shows knowledge and understanding of the nutrition and uses of pulses. It would access higher band marks.

Weaker answer

Pulses are very good for you. They are eaten mainly by vegetarians instead of meat. You will find them in ready-made vegetarian meals like curry or chilli. You can add pulses to stews. They are cheap.

Commentary

This is a low level answer. The student has made basic statements but these need justifying, with examples, to show clearly that they have good knowledge, e.g. the first sentence could give examples of pulses and how they may be used. There are no references to the nutritional values found in pulses or vegetarian/vegan diets.

SECTION 3

BUTTER, OIL, MARGARINE, SUGAR AND SYRUP

 Target: I need to be able to understand and write about...

Types of fats available

Nutritional values

Science of fats

Uses of fats in cooking

BUTTER, OIL AND MARGARINE

Effect of heat on fats

Composition of fats

Extra information may be found in the textbook pages 336–347.

Types of fats available

Fats tend to be firm, solid or hard at room temperature, whereas oils are liquid. Fats can come from both animal and plant sources.

ANIMAL FAT

  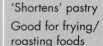 

	BUTTER	**GHEE**	**LARD**	**SUET**
DESCRIPTION	Made from churning milk to separate out and solidify the cream into butterfat	Made by removing the milk solids from butter, producing a clear fat	Made from rendered pig fat	Hard fat surrounding kidneys of cows and sheep. The fat is shredded into thin strands
USES	Adds flavour and colour to baked foods. Must be mixed with oil when frying to prevent burning	Used widely in Indian cooking for frying and gives food a nutty flavour	'Shortens' pastry. Good for frying/roasting foods	Suet pastry, steamed puddings and dumplings

VEGETABLE FAT

MARGARINE

SPREADS

TREX/COOKEEN

	MARGARINE	SPREADS	TREX/COOKEEN
DESCRIPTION	Vegetable oils are **hydrogenated** to form a solid fat	Margarine blended with vegetable oil so it remains soft and spreadable	Vegetable oils are hydrogenated to form a solid, white fat
USES	Baking and as a butter alternative	Spreading on bread and baking	A lard alternative for pastry

Oils

Oils come from different plant sources such as sunflowers, rapeseed, maize and soya beans. 'Vegetable' oil is a blend of different oils. Most oils cope well with high heats for frying and roasting. Oils from walnuts, avocados, almonds, sesame and flax seeds add flavour when used in salad dressings and marinades, and when sautéing vegetables.

Nutritional values

Fats and oils are extremely energy dense at 9kcal [37kJ] per gram or 120kcals per tablespoon and should not be over-consumed because they will cause weight gain, obesity and coronary heart disease. To reduce fat intake choose lean meats and low fat products, eat fewer ready-prepared foods, don't fry or roast foods and do snack on fruit and vegetables rather than crisps, chips and sausage rolls. Some fats and most oils do provide us with 'good' omega 3 and omega 6 fatty acids, and vitamins A, D, E and K.

Grade boost

Learn these key words and use them in your written work as this will show you understand the question:

Anti-oxidant

Double bond

Hydrogenated

Shortening

quickfire

1 Name two dishes that each animal and vegetable fat can be used in.

quickfire

2 Find out which three cuts of meat have the least fat per 100g.
3 How many grams of fat are in 100g of the following:
   a) crisps
   b) chips
   c) carrots
   d) apples?
4 Name two fats containing omega 3 and/or omega 6 fatty acids.

▼ Steamed steak pudding

Science of fats

Fats are classified into saturated and unsaturated depending how the atoms of carbon, hydrogen and oxygen are structured.

Saturated fats have all the carbon atoms in each molecule joined (saturated) with hydrogen atoms.

1. Found mainly in animal fats and linked with raised LDL (low density lipoprotein) cholesterol levels.
2. Associated with coronary heart disease.
3. Examples are butter, ghee, cream, cheese and meat fat.

Monounsaturated fat has **one** carbon atom in each molecule joined to one other carbon atom, forming a **double bond**.

1. The double bond blocks any hydrogen molecule from joining the two carbon atoms.
2. This fat helps to reduce LDL (bad) blood cholesterol and increases HDL (high density lipoprotein) (good) blood cholesterol.
3. Examples come from some plant oils such as olive and rapeseed oils.

Polyunsaturated fat is where several carbon atoms form double bonds reducing the hydrogen atoms available in the molecule.

1. This provides HDL (good) cholesterol and is a good source of omega 3 fatty acids.
2. Examples are sunflower, soya bean and corn oils.

quickfire

5 Can you name one fat from each of the three different types?

Grade boost

Learn the differences between saturated, monounsaturated and polyunsaturated fats.

Grade boost

Learn and understand the terms 'LDL' and 'HDL'.

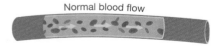
Normal blood flow

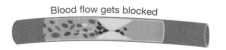
Blood flow gets blocked

▲ Can you see how fat can cause blockages in our blood vessels?

Cholesterol is a fatty substance produced by our livers and found in many foods. Raised cholesterol levels in the bloodstream can cause arteries to block. LDL cholesterol is unhealthy and its intake should be reduced. HDL cholesterol is a healthier type of fat, which helps to reduce the risk of heart attacks and strokes.

Hydrogenation

Oils are hydrogenated to change them from a liquid to a firm fat. Hydrogen atoms in unsaturated fats are forced to join the double bonded carbon atoms, creating a hard vegetable fat.

Rancidity

Fats and oils are affected by temperature and oxygen, which makes them 'go off'. Fat molecules will break down causing the flavours to become unpleasant. **Anti-oxidants** are added to some fats and oils during processing to prevent rancidity.

Plasticity

Different fats melt at different temperatures. We use these characteristics to help us when preparing foods, for example butter needs to be at room temperature to easily spread on bread but cold and firm for 'rubbing in'.

Aeration

While creaming fat with sugar, air particles become trapped, which helps to create a stable foam.

Uses of fats in cooking

Fats add colour, flavour and texture to food. They also help to extend the shelf life of ready-made products.

COLOUR

Butter and margarine give a golden colour to cakes, biscuits and pastries.

FLAVOUR

Butter gives all baked products a rich flavour.

TEXTURE

The 'melt-in-the-mouth', crumbly texture of pastry and biscuits is due to the shortening action of fats. They help to provide a soft texture in cake making. Oil contributes to the crunchy surface of fried foods.

EMULSIONS

Oils and vinegar mixed to make salad dressings will separate. Whisking a little egg yolk to the oil and vinegar will create a stable emulsion – mayonnaise.

Effect of heat on fats

The melting points of fats and oils vary according to their types of fatty acid. If over-heated, fats and oils give off a blue smoke, called the 'smoke point', and then at the 'flash point' will spontaneously ignite.

Cooking oil	Smoke point
Canola oil unrefined	107°C
Extra virgin olive oil	160°C
Canola oil refined	204°C
Grapeseed oil	204°C
Virgin olive oil	216°C
Peanut oil	231°C
Sesame oil refined	232°C
Soya bean oil	257°C
Corn oil	236°C
Avocado oil	271°C

quickfire

6   What is the 'flash point' for butter and sunflower oil?

7   Why does fat extend the shelf life of ready-made products?

8   Which fat gives shortcrust pastry the melt-in-the mouth texture?

SECTION 3

Types of sugar and sweetener

SUGAR AND OTHER SWEETENERS

Nutritional values

Science of sugar

Uses of sugars

 Extra information may be found in the textbook pages 348–361.

Types of sugar and sweetener

Honey, fruits and sugars have always been used to sweeten and preserve foods. In the last 50 years the consumption of sugar and sugary foods has risen enormously.

Sugar

All sugar is processed from sugar cane or sugar beet producing sweet liquids, which are then refined into molasses and syrup, or dried into crystals.

Grade boost

Learn these key words and use them in your written work as this will show you understand the question:

Disaccharides

Monosaccharides

What is this plant? ▲

Free sugars

Sucrose, glucose, honey, fructose and glucose syrup are all classed as free sugars or NMEs (non-milk extrinsic sugars).

quickfire

9   How many kcals are there in one teaspoon of sugar?

10 Which sugar crop is grown widely in the UK?

Are these two sweeteners 'free sugars'? ▲

Type of sugar	Description	Uses
Granulated	Rough, gritty white glucose crystals	In hot drinks and to sweeten cooked fruit
Caster	Fine, white glucose crystals, which easily dissolve	Cake and biscuit making
Icing	Fine, white glucose powder	Icings and buttercream
Soft brown	Fine, brown crystals formed from the sweet sugar cane molasses	Gingerbreads, fudge, toffee, some marinades
Demerara	Rough, gritty brown glucose and molasses crystals	In coffee and some cake recipes
Muscovado	A mix of refined and unrefined molasses sugar	Rich fruit cakes

Syrups	Description	Uses
Golden syrup	Refined syrup formed by heating sugar + water	Cakes made by the melting method, in caramel
Black treacle	Thick, dark-coloured molasses syrup with a strong flavour	Gingerbread and rich fruit cakes
Maple syrup	A thin syrup from the maple tree	Poured over fruit and ice cream

Honey

Bees use flower nectar to produce honey to feed bees in the hive. The flavour and consistency varies depending on the flower nectar used, for example clover honey is thick and spreadable whereas orange blossom honey is usually runny. Honey can be used to sweeten drinks, put on breakfast cereals, spread on toast and to cure hams.

quickfire

11 Why don't vegans eat honey?

▲ How would you use this honey?

▲ Why might people needing to lose weight use this?

Sweeteners

These are synthetic, artificial sweeteners containing almost no kcals. They are used to replace sugars and syrups in foods and drinks but tend to leave an aftertaste in the mouth. Popular sweeteners are 'Splenda', 'Sweetex', and 'Candarel'. They are inexpensive compared to the cost of sugar, so are now widely used in food manufacturing. However, some people think that sweeteners are not good for you.

SECTION 3

Science of sugar

Sugar molecules are composed of **monosaccharides** or **disaccharides**.

Monosaccharides are single molecules of sugar, for example:

- Fructose sugars are found in fruit, vegetables and honey.
- Glucose sugars are synthesised from some fruit and vegetables.
- Galactose sugars are found in milk sugar lactose.

Disaccharides have two molecules linked together, for example:

- Sucrose is glucose + fructose combined = granulated sugar.
- Lactose is glucose + galactose combined; found in milk.
- Maltose is two molecules of glucose joined together.

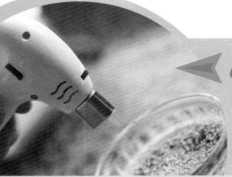

Caramelisation

Sugars caramelise and turn brown on heating, giving cakes and biscuits their distinctive colour and flavour. By using heat, sugar can be melted to form shapes and shards, which harden on cooling.

Raising agent

Sugar helps to trap air, which aerates and increases the volume of a dish.

- Sugar + butter traps air when creamed for a Victoria sandwich.
- Sugar + egg white traps air when whisked for meringues.

Preservation

Foods stored in strong sugar solutions will have long shelf lives because bacteria, yeasts and moulds cannot grow in this extreme sugary environment, for example jams and chutneys.

Fermentation

A small amount of sugar added to a yeasted dough will make the yeast work to speed up the production of CO_2.

Foaming

Sugar helps to stabilise aerated foams such as meringue mixtures.

Enzymic browning

Sugar added to cooked fruits stops oxygen browning the cut surface of the fruits.

Sweeteners are intensely sweet, synthetic substances that mimic the sweetness of sugar. Unlike sugar they do not easily melt and produce dense, dry and lumpy cakes and biscuits.

Boiling temperature	Properties	Uses
104°C	Large gloss	Jam, marmalade, jelly
107°C	Thread	Sugar syrups, some icings, Italian meringues
115°C	Soft ball	Fudge, fondants
118–121°C	Hard ball	Caramels, nougat, soft toffee
138°C	Crack	Toffee
143–149°C	Hard crack	Butterscotch, nut brittle, barley sugar
155–190°C	Caramel	For lining dishes and moulds; colouring sauces, soups

Nutritional values

The average person eats about 38kg of sugar each year. Sugar has no nutritional benefits because there are no essential vitamins, minerals or proteins present. Sugar is 4kcal (17kJ) per gram of energy and if not used up it becomes body fat leading to weight gain, obesity, type 2 diabetes and coronary heart disease. Sugar can also cause tooth decay and gum disease.

Most factory-made food products such as ready-made meals, ketchup, yoghurts, bread and breakfast cereals contain 'hidden sugars', making it is easy to over-consume sugar without realising.

quickfire

12 Why is sugar referred to as 'empty calories'?

Uses

Sugar is used to sweeten, and add colour and texture to foods such as cakes, pastries and biscuits.

Krisp-es

NUTRITION FACTS

Serving size		25g
Calories:		124

% Daily Value*

Total fat	1.7g	3%
Saturated fat	1g	5%
Cholesterol	0mg	1%
Sodium	8g	8%
Total carbohydrate	12g	4%
Dietary fibre	3g	9%
Sugar	14.4g	12%
Protein	4g	9%

Vitamin A	0%	Vitamin C	2%
Calcium	4%	Iron	25%

*Percent Daily Values are based on a 2,000 calorie diet. Your daily values may be higher or lower depending on your calorie needs.

EXAM QUESTIONS

1 State the main difference between a fat and an oil.

_____

_____

_____

2 State two sources of essential fatty acids.

[i] _____

_____

[ii] _____

3 Why is butter not recommended for frying?

_____

_____

_____

_____

_____

4 What is meant by 'smoke point'?

_____

_____

_____

_____

_____

_____

_____

_____

_____

_____

_____

5 Name one monosaccharide.

_____

6 Name one disaccharide.

_____

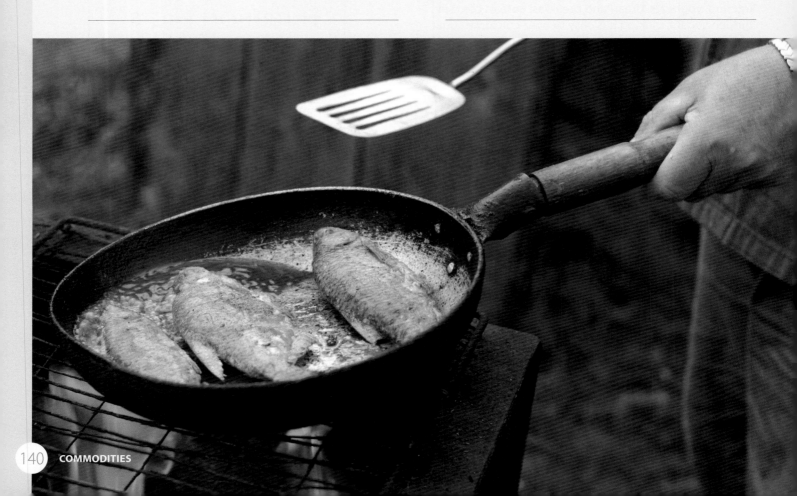

Sample exam questions and answers with commentaries

Q1 Explain how fats and oils are used during food preparation and cooking.

Model answer

If the recipe calls for a hard fat you would choose butter, margarine and/or lard. If an oil you would use sunflower oil or melted butter/margarine. Hard fats such as butter and lard are rubbed into flour to make pastry short and crumbly, whereas soft butter or margarine is used in creamed cakes because the fat will trap air into the mixture. All fats add moisture and shelf life to baked goods, e.g. a fatless sponge stales very quickly compared to a creamed Victoria sandwich. Butter gives a rich flavour to cakes and biscuits. Sunflower oil is needed for frying rather than butter because vegetable oils can safely reach high cooking temperatures. Frying in oil gives food a crunchy texture and a golden colour. Most salad dressings use vegetable oils to give a mild flavour or a nut oil, such as walnut oil, to give a more definite flavour.

Commentary

This is a very good answer that would access the higher marks available. The uses of fats and oils in both preparation and cooking have been discussed. Examples of foods/dishes have also been stated.

Weaker answer

Fats and oils are used in all sorts of cooking, e.g. oil to fry chips or butter to make pastry. Blocks of fat must be stored in the fridge. You shouldn't eat too much fatty food because they are bad for your health.

Commentary

This is a very limited answer that would only access low band marks because it does not show the student's understanding of fats and oils. Read the model answer to see how many more points could have been included.

The last point made is irrelevant to this question.

Q2 What are the differences between a sugar and a sweetener?

Model answer

Sugar comes from processing sugar cane or sugar beet and is considered a 'natural' product, whereas most sweeteners are a combination of synthetic molecules mimicking the sweetness of sugar. Sweeteners, like sugar, sweeten cups of tea and are in bottles of squash and fizzy drinks. You cannot easily cook with sweeteners because they don't have the same amount of 'bulk' as sugar and they react differently to heat. They don't melt or combine easily with other ingredients. Cakes made using sweeteners will be dry and dense.

Commentary

This answer would access the higher band marks. It is quite a difficult question to answer so this is a fairly good response. The student has successfully compared and contrasted sugar and sweetener with reference to sources, uses and taste.

Weaker answer

Sugar is a natural ingredient but sweeteners are a bunch of chemicals. Sugars taste sweet and are bad for you. Sweeteners have a funny sweet tang. Sweeteners are used by people wanting to lose weight. They are in lots of foods.

Commentary

This student has a basic knowledge of sugars and sweeteners. There is an attempt at comparing and contrasting sugar with sweetener but it is limited. This would be awarded low marks.

Principles of Nutrition (page 18)

1 growth/repair/cell maintenance

2 High biological value: proteins that contain all the essential amino acids that the body cannot make. Found in dairy foods, meat, fish, eggs and soya.

3 soya/tofu/quinoa/beans/peas/lentils/nuts

4 Keeps us warm/insulates the body.

Provides vitamins A, D, E and K.

Contains essential fatty acids, which the body can't make.

Protects vital organs – heart, liver, kidneys.

Important for our hormone production.

5 Eating too much fat regularly can lead to several health issues such as becoming overweight or obese, and developing coronary heart disease because arteries become blocked. It can also cause liver damage and bad breath.

6 'Hidden' fats refers to any fat in foods that are not obvious, e.g. cheese contains 20–30% fat but most people wouldn't know this because it is 'hidden' in the cheese. Also, pies and cakes contain hidden fats because they cannot be seen.

7 Fats come in different types and you need to choose the correct one for the job.

When frying use sunflower oil or lard because they can reach high temperatures before burning.

A mix of lard/white fat and hard margarine or butter is used when making pastry. The lard/white fat gives the 'short' texture and the butter adds colour and flavour.

Soft margarines are ideal for cake making because they 'cream' with the caster sugar very easily.

Suet is a hard shredded fat that is ideal for making steamed puddings, which need long cooking times.

Olive oil, walnut oil and sesame oil are ideal for salad dressings because they add flavour.

8 It is important to ensure the body can easily remove waste products (faeces). It also helps regulate blood sugar levels and can keep us feeling fuller for longer, which contributes to maintaining a healthy weight.

A diet low in dietary fibre can result in constipation, piles and, eventually, bowel problems that could result in some cancers.

9 Fat soluble vitamins: A, D, E, K

Water soluble vitamins: B group, C

10 A diet lacking in vitamin C can result in wounds not healing quickly and bleeding gums. Iron would not be easily absorbed, which can lead to tiredness.

11 Vitamin B12 is found mainly in red meat, especially liver, and dairy foods. Because vegans don't eat animal products they must find vegetable sources of B12, e.g. fortified breakfast cereals and soya milk.

12 Don't add salt at the table.

Cook from scratch rather than rely on ready-made meals.

Snack on fruit or vegetables rather than crisps.

Use herbs in cooking to replace salt.

Use lo-salt and products that have reduced salt content.

13 Iron is vital for the formation of haemoglobin, which carries oxygen around the body. A lack of iron will cause anaemia. Vitamin C in the diet is vital to make sure the body can absorb any iron present. So a lack of vitamin C means that iron cannot be absorbed.

Iron is found in red meat and green, leafy vegetables. Vitamin C is found in tomatoes, citrus fruits and red peppers. A good meal could be: steak pie, new potatoes and sprouts with a glass of orange juice.

Diet and Good Health (page 24)

1 The Eatwell Guide illustrates the different percentages of food groups, e.g. 1/3 of our food should come from fruit and vegetables and we should eat fats and oils sparingly.

Eight top tips highlights the eight guidelines for healthy eating. They include basing our meals on starchy foods and fruit and vegetables, eating less salt and fatty foods, and drinking plenty of water.

Five-a-day. By eating at least five vegetables and fruit a day for good health.

2 Energy dense refers to foods that contain lots of kcal per gram such as fats and oils which have 9kcal per 1 gram.

3 The body will not have received any food for at least eight hours and will need fuel for energy to kick-start the day. People who skip breakfast tend to have poor concentration in the mornings and risk snacking on unhealthy foods mid-morning.

4 This person should maintain a healthy weight, which helps balance their blood sugar levels. They need to eat wholegrain cereals, rice or pasta and wholemeal bread to provide slow release energy. They must limit eating sugary, fatty foods and increase their vegetable intake.

5 Preparing:

Choose lean cuts of meat, e.g. chicken breast rather than lamb chops.

Grill, oven bake or boil foods rather than roasting or frying them.

Dry-fry foods rather than deep fry.

Cut off the fat before cooking or before serving.

Use low-cal sprays when frying.

Use skimmed milk, reduced fat cheese and other reduced fat products.

6 Vegetarian meals must use a wide range of foods including peas, beans, nuts, lentils and soya products as well as a range of fruit and vegetables. Many vegetarians eat dairy products but they must be sure they don't eat too many each day so that the fat levels are kept low. Vegetarians must not base their meals on one type of food.

7 From fruit and grains: LBV protein/vitamin C/fibre/B vitamins/carbohydrates/fat

From milk or natural yoghurt (to go with the cereal): HBV proteins/calcium/fat/carbohydrates/vitamins A and D

The Science of Cooking Food (page 32)

1 To soften it, e.g. stewing steak.

To make it safe to eat, e.g. chicken.

To reduce bulk, e.g. cabbage.

To make it digestible, e.g. pastry.

To improve the flavour, e.g. casseroles.

To provide different textures, e.g. crunchy toast and soft boiled egg.

To provide hot food in cold weather, e.g. stews.

To make it look more appealing, e.g. roasted meat.

2 Hot water or air molecules rise from the bottom of the pan of liquid or oven to the top where they cool slightly before falling back to the bottom to be heated. The process starts over again. Heat is transferred to the food by the movement of these heated molecules.

3 Heat is transferred to the food by direct contact with a hot surface, e.g. an egg on the hot surface of a frying pan.

4 Starch molecules become soft and absorb water when heated in a liquid. At 60°C+ the starch molecules swell and eventually burst causing the liquid to thicken. This process is call gelatinisation.

5 When egg whites are whisked the mechanical action aerates and increases the volume of the whites because the albumen proteins unravel and denature making the egg white foam stiff.

6 warmth/food/time/oxygen/correct pH

7 bicarbonate of soda

8 When rubbing in the fat particles coat the flour grains to prevent too much water absorption. This prevents the gluten forming. During rolling out the gluten is stretched, which sets on cooking.

9 When pasta is put into boiling water the dry, starch molecules soften, absorbing water. The pasta changes from dry and brittle becoming softer and chewy. Cooking makes the pasta digestible.

Food Spoilage (page 40)

1 Salmonella/E. coli/Staphylococcus A./Campylobacte/

2 It is where one bacterium divides into two bacteria. Each bacterium is identical.

3 Cross-contamination happens when bacteria are moved from one place to another by humans, equipment, pests and insects.

To prevent this always keep food covered and wash hands before and after handling food. Equipment and surfaces must be washed and sanitised after use.

4 HACCP stands for hazard analysis critical control point. Food companies must have a HACCP in place ensuring any potential hazards are controlled, preventing foods becoming unsafe to eat. For example, make sure that high risk foods are stored in a fridge at 5°C to slow the rate of bacterial growth.

5 Foods must be stored correctly. High risk foods in a fridge at 5°C to slow down the rate of bacterial growth. Ambient foods must be stored in sealed containers to prevent contamination. Freshly cooked foods, e.g. a cake, must be covered until it is cool enough to go into a sealed tin.

Food handlers must observe personal hygiene rules – hands washed, hair back, no coughing or spitting.

During cooking make sure that high risk foods reach a core temperature of at least 75°C.

Never reheat foods more than once.

Don't put warm or hot foods into a fridge.

6 a) A foil dish with a card lid or plastic container with a tight fitting lid.

It makes sure the food doesn't leak and these materials are easily written on.

b) Foil/paper bag/greaseproof paper and bag.

The sandwich can be wrapped tightly in the material keeping the filling secure.

The material moulds to the sandwich.

Foil will keep the heat in.

7 Reducing food waste: Only buy and cook what is needed. Cook to order, so that less food is wasted. Don't have too varied a menu. The more foods on a menu means the caterer will have to stock a lot of perishable foods. Re-use left overs e.g. cooked vegetables into a soup and bread crusts into a bread and butter pudding or into breadcrumbs.

Reducing non-food waste: To save water use an efficient dishwasher rather than washing up under a running tap. Turn off grills, hobs and oven when not needed or only switch them on when needed. Turn off lights and fans when not needed.

Reducing packaging waste: Buy large boxes of foods to minimise packaging waste, e.g. 1kg bag of sugar to fill the sugar bowls rather than using individual sachets. Buy unpackaged fruit and vegetables. Buy meat and fish locally, where it is wrapped in one plastic bag rather than sealed plastic boxes. Recycle all packaging and use recycled packaging where possible.

Food Provenance and Food Waste (page 46)

1 To keep food safe from contamination.

To increase shelf life.

Keeps fragile foods safe, e.g. peaches, which bruise easily.

Has important information for the consumer such as nutritional details and cooking instructions.

2 It is strong.

It can be lightweight.

It can be moulded into different shapes.

It protects the food from contamination.

It can be vacuum sealed giving a very long shelf life.

It can be recycled.

3 Glass packaging is very heavy and bulky compared to metal and paperboard packaging and it will cost manufacturers more to transport their goods around the country.

Glass jars and bottles are easily smashed in transit, which can affect business costs and can also be dangerous.

4 Food provenance has become very important to the consumer because many people now want to know exactly where their foods originate from. This is especially important to customers who wish to source local foods. The provenance may indicate whether foods are seasonal or 'forced' in heated poly-tunnels.

5 Food sustainability is where foods are grown with the least impact on the environment. This type of food production must use fewer natural resources than traditionally produced food.

6 Plan the week's menus to prevent buying too much food.

Use an accurate shopping list and stick to it.

Only buy what you need – don't be tempted with BOGOF or three for two offers unless they are products you will definitely use.

Don't go shopping when you are hungry because you end up buying more food than you actually need.

Cook from scratch rather than relying on ready-made foods.

Use leftovers for another meal, e.g. yesterday's roast chicken in a salad today.

Freeze leftovers to use in another meal.

7 You will save money because every piece of food thrown away has cost money. For example, a loaf of bread cost £1 but 1/3 of the loaf became mouldy so had to be thrown away. In real terms 33p was thrown in the bin. Nobody would empty their purses into the bin but this is what you are doing when you throw food away. This is one reason it is important to use up all foods rather than throw them away.

8 Food poverty is where a person:

a. does not have access to affordable healthy foods

b. simply cannot afford to buy nourishing foods

c. lacks the skills and knowledge to make healthy meals.

9 They could walk to the local shops which avoids using a car. Buy locally grown/reared seasonal produce because the food miles will be quite small, e.g. local grown runner beans rather than buying Kenyan beans.

Have the shopping delivered. One supermarket delivery van delivering to 12 houses will prevent 12 car journeys to and from the supermarket.

Technological Developments (page 56)

1 Protect the food/stop it becoming damaged.

Prevent contamination.

Extend the shelf life (MAP).

Makes it easier to transport.

Provide consumers with information.

2 MAP packaging has had the 'air' inside the container altered to a mix of CO_2 and nitrogen. These gases slow down the natural decaying process. A good example is that strawberries last longer on the supermarket shelf.

3 Hydroponics is where crops are not grown in soil but in some kind of water solution. The farmer is able to get greater yields of crops than through the traditional soil method. Examples are lettuces and tomatoes.

4 Functional foods are those that have increased nutrition or are developed around a specific function such as milk and yoghurt that contain stanols and sterols, which can help reduce a person's cholesterol. So these products can be used to improve a diet.

5 Foods are fortified to either replace nutrients lost during processing or to add a nutrient to a food. This makes sure that consumers receive the nutrients to prevent deficiency. Examples are:

- breakfast cereals fortified with B vitamins
- bread fortified with folic acid
- margarines fortified with vitamin D.

6 Faster working than humans.

Fewer errors and mistakes – removes human error.

More hygienic than humans – as long as the machines are cleaned and sanitised after use.

All products can be made safely, efficiently and with good consistency.

7 These symbols are quality assurance marks that give the consumer confidence that the foods have been grown or reared with clear, controlled regulations. The red tractor means that all the food originates from trustworthy sources. Fairtrade means that farmers and their workers receive decent wages and work conditions. The Soil Association sets and certifies organic status for crops and animals.

8 People are working longer hours so don't have time to cook from scratch in the evenings, resulting in the growth of ready-made/cook–chill meals. In the evenings families may not all be at home at the same time, due to parents coming in late from work and teenagers having clubs to attend. Therefore, families often eat in isolation using individual portion ready-meals that can simply be heated in the microwave oven. Many people do not know how to cook because they have never had the time to learn, so rely on convenience foods.

9 People are concerned about excess packaging and packaging waste, so consumers expect manufacturers to use minimal packaging that is recyclable. Lots of plastic is used, which consumers expect to be biodegradable. So, manufacturers must consider these points when developing a new product. Can the foods be developed in eco-factories that use solar and wind generated power?

The origins and quality of the foods must be considered, e.g. will the manufacturer use chicken that is 'mass' produced in Asia or chicken that is sourced locally? British reared chicken will be 'greener' than chickens flown 8000 miles from the Far East. This same dilemma affects all food products used by manufacturers. Consumers are looking for more environmentally friendly foods that the manufacturer needs to consider during food development stages.

Factors Affecting Food Choice (page 64)

1 Consumers often choose to buy seasonal fruit and vegetables because they are more easily available, may be cheaper, will be richer in nutrition and will taste much better than buying the same food out of season.

2 An intolerance causes discomfort and unpleasant symptoms, e.g. skin rash or bloating and diarrhoea. If the person stops eating the cause (e.g. bread) the symptoms improve. It is not usually life threatening.

An allergy is much more serious and can result in death. Allergens include peanuts, shellfish, strawberries.

3 The manufacturers will set up a panel of tasters who will provide the sensory information about the product. To do this the taster panel needs to understand what they have to do. Each taster will receive the same sized portion of food in identical containers. They may be assessing more than one product using a triangle test to see if they can tell the difference or they might use a rating test where the panel marks the food out of 5. The tasters must be given a wide range of sensory descriptors to help their analyses.

The manufacturer might focus on just flavour or it might be flavour AND texture.

The tasters should be given water in between tasting and shouldn't taste too many products.

4 Sensory analysis is really important to the manufacturer to ensure the product will sell and be successful. The product must look good, have a good mouth feel and have a good balance and richness of flavours.

5 Market research informs the manufacturer if people will actually buy the newly developed product. If the consumer doesn't like it the product won't sell and this will be very costly to the manufacturer.

The market researchers ask consumers to assess how the food looks, smells and tastes. Mouth feel is very important too.

6 There are many factors affecting our food choices.

Whether we are lacto-vegetarian, vegan or omnivore determines where we source our protein foods.

The types of foods eaten as we grow up set our pattern of food choices, e.g. if you never ate fish growing up the likelihood is that you won't eat it in adulthood because you 'don't like it.

Our income determines the type of food we buy.

Facilities in your kitchen, e.g. if you don't own a freezer you can't buy frozen foods.

Culture impacts the foods purchased. Different communities often open shops selling their cultural foods so that they can purchase ingredients they are used to, although the major supermarkets are now including cultural products on their shelves.

The time of the year affects food choice. Stews and casseroles are usually eaten in the winter, whereas salad foods tend to be eaten in the summer.

Cereals (page 82)

1 [i] Endosperm

[ii] Bran

[iii] Germ

2 starch carbohydrate/protein/B vitamins/calcium/iron

3 rye/barley/oats/rice/maize/quinoa/arrowroot/tapioca/sago

4 The Chorleywood process reduces the manufacturing time, allowing the manufacturer to make each loaf much more quickly than using the traditional method of bread-making. It involves adding vitamin C to the bread mix and uses high intensity kneading, developing the gluten structure very quickly.

The other benefit to the manufacturer is that more money can be made because they are making many more loaves per day compared to a traditional baker.

5 Use wholemeal, wholegrain or granary flour. Add nuts, seeds or dried fruit.

6 Because it contains higher levels of the protein gluten. During kneading and proving the gluten must be strong enough to be stretched. That is why strong flour must be used.

7 a) roux sauce/bechamel sauce

b) toast/tea cakes/the surface of cakes and biscuits

c) bread/cakes

8 Yeast is a living organism which will reproduce and give off CO_2 in the right conditions. Yeast needs warmth (37°C), moisture, food, oxygen and time to grow. During proving the yeast in the dough is given the ideal conditions so it ferments producing CO_2. The gas bubbles given off expand and inflate the dough causing the bread dough to rise.

9 Dextrins are formed.

Starch dextrinises.

Surface changes colour due to dextrins forming – golden brown.

Flavour changes due to dextrins forming – sweet, nutty flavour.

10 The bread has been grilled or toasted. The surface carbohydrate has become crisp, a golden colour and will have a sweet, nutty taste due to dextrins being formed by the heat from the grill.

Fruit and Vegetables (page 94)

1 Fruit: oranges, grapefruit, strawberries, kiwi, papaya

Vegetables: peas, tomatoes, peppers, broccoli, new potatoes

2 To help the body get rid of faeces (poo) easily and help prevent bowel disease and some cancers.

3 Early crop: Jersey Royals, Pentland Javelin, Arran Pilot

Main crop: Cara, Desiree, King Edwards, Maris Piper, pink fir apple

4 You need a main crop potato such as King Edwards. Peel thinly and cut into chunks. They could be parboiled in salted water for five minutes (but you don't have to do this). Drain them and let the surface dry off. Heat some oil/dripping in a roasting tin. Place the dry potato pieces in the hot fat and baste each potato.

Place in a hot oven: gas 6/20°C for 45–60 minutes. Regularly baste the potatoes to get a crisp surface.

5 Most fruit and vegetables need to be stored in a dark, cool, dry place. Soft fruits and vegetables, e.g. berries and salad veg, should be stored in the salad drawer in a fridge. Muddy potatoes last longer if they are left muddy and not washed before storing.

6 Fruit and vegetables can spoil quite quickly due to moulds and yeasts. To prevent them going off they need to be preserved.

Freezing: many fruits/vegetables are prepared for use then blanched in boiling hot water for one minute then into cold water to chill them. They need to be dried, placed into freezer bags and frozen quickly.

Chutney: cut veg into small pieces and cook in spiced vinegar until the vegetables are soft and the liquid has evaporated. Pour the chutney into very hot jars and seal them immediately.

Jam: soften the fruit until cooked. Add the required amount of sugar and cook on a low heat to dissolve the sugar. Boil to the jam setting point, 105°C, pour into very hot jars and seal the lids tightly.

7 Both batons and julienne cuts are the same length. The difference is that julienne are narrower than batons. Batons can be about 3–4mm wide whereas julienne are 1–2mm wide.

8 Fruit and vegetables are very versatile because there is a wide range available. If you are cooking a quick stir fry you would use vegetables that cook very quickly, e.g. sugarsnap peas and peppers. For a stew you would use vegetables that take longer to cook but don't fall apart such as carrot and swede. Some vegetables can be served raw in salads such as grated carrot, diced peppers and slices of tomato.

Fruit is often served raw in dessert such as the berries, bananas and kiwi fruit. Bramley apples are excellent for making pies and they go well with raspberries or plums. Fruit can be added to savoury dishes such as apricots to a lamb tagine or pineapple to a sweet and sour sauce.

9 Fruit and vegetables tend to be cheaper in season and more readily available because they will have been grown in the UK. This avoids contributing to a large carbon footprint that imported produce has. They also tend to taste better when in season and have increased nutrition too.

10 Rich, vibrant green colour/firm and crisp/not soft or 'bendy'

Milk, Cheese and Yoghurt (page 108)

1 Provides protein for growth.

Good source of calcium.

Aids strong bones/bone development.

Aids strong teeth.

Helps prevent rickets.

Assists in functioning of muscles and nerves.

2 lactose intolerance

3 In a cool, dark place. Ideally, in a fridge at 5°C. The lid must be firmly attached to the milk container. Never mix old milk with new milk. Do not leave milk in sunlight.

4 protein/fat/carbohydrate (lactose)/B vitamins/vitamin A/vitamin D/phosphorous/sodium/potassium

5 dried/UHT/long life/condensed/evaporated

6 Cows are milked twice a day using specialised machinery. The milk is stored in large, refrigerated, large vats. This is known as raw milk and needs to be processed to make it safe to drink. The milk is heated to 75°C for about 25 seconds. This is called pasteurisation and ensures that harmful bacteria are killed.

The fat can be skimmed away to create skimmed or semi-skimmed milk.

Whole milk can be homogenised where the milk is forced through a fine mesh to break up the milk fat (cream). This results in the fat being spread throughout the milk.

7 tuberculosis/tuberculinum

8 Slows down growth of bacteria.

To keep it safe/cold.

Keeps longer.

Prevents it going off/mouldy.

9 soft: Brie, Camembert, feta

hard: Cheddar, Red Leicester, parmesan, Manchego

blue: Stilton, Danish Blue, Gorgonzola

10 Cheese can be made more digestible by cutting into small pieces, slicing or grating it. Heating cheese also makes it more digestible. But if it is over-cooked it becomes more indigestible.

11 Cheese melts at about 65°C causing it to become soft and spreadable. Some cheeses become stringy at this point, e.g. mozzarella. The fat is released and can create an oily surface on the cheese. However, too much heat will cause the proteins to harden and become tough.

Meat, Poultry and Chicken (page 122)

1 red meat: beef, lamb, pork, venison, horsemeat, goat

poultry: chicken, turkey, duck, goose, quail, pheasant

2 vitamins A, D, B and B12/iron/magnesium/selenium/zinc

3 B12 keeps the nerves and blood cells healthy. It prevents pernicious anaemia, extreme tiredness and confusion.

4 We are advised to reduce our fat intake to prevent weight gain, blocked arteries and developing heart disease. One way of achieving this is to eat lean meat so buy 5% fat minced beef, trim off meat fat before cooking or eating it.

5 protein, fat/omega 6/zinc/potassium/sodium/vitamins A and D

6 Fish can be stored in a freezer at −18°C to stop bacterial growth. It can be pickled in vinegar, such as soused herring. The altered pH will prevent bacterial growth. Fish can be sealed in jars and cans, which extend the shelf life. Fish that is smoked will have a longer shelf life.

Eggs (page 124)

1 quail/duck/goose/ostrich

2 albumen

3 protein/fat

4 aeration/glazing/emulsifying/coating/binding/thickening/enriching/garnishing

5 poaching/frying/scrambling/baking/boiling

6 Egg white can trap lots of air when whisked. The volume increases as the foam is created. The protein molecules unravel, denaturing, and form a network around the air molecules and so the foam is formed.

7 Egg white foam will fail if there is even the tiniest molecule of fat, oil or egg yolk present. So the beaters and bowl must be absolutely clean and grease free.

8 a) Beaten egg coats the meat, which helps the breadcrumbs to stick to the meat. During cooking the egg protein coagulates, sealing the food and forming a crispy coating.

b) Oil and vinegar will not mix but by adding egg yolk, which contains lecithin, will emulsify the oil and vinegar creating a stable emulsion.

c) Beaten egg brushed over the raw pastry creates a coating which, when heated, will give the pastry a golden shine.

Beans, Nuts, Seeds, Soya, Tofu and Mycoprotein (page 130)

1 peas/beans/lentils/nuts/tofu/Quorn/quinoa/soya

2 Low biological value proteins. These are protein foods that do not contain all the essential amino acids.

3 soya bean

4 Two LBV proteins are used in the same meal, which form a HBV protein meal, e.g. beans on toast – the proteins in the beans and the proteins in the bread together make a HBV dish.

5 beans on toast/nut roast with bean salad/vegetarian chilli sin carne/hummus, hummus and salad

6 Lacto-vegetarians eat dairy products but do not eat meat, fish and eggs.

Ovo-lacto vegetarians eat dairy and egg products but do not eat meat or fish.

Vegans do not eat any animal products including honey.

Butter, Oil, Margarine, Sugar and Syrup (page 140)

1 At room temperature a fat is firm or solid, whereas an oil is liquid.

2 salmon/sardines/rapeseed oil/olive oil/sunflower oil/sunflower seeds/pumpkin seeds/soya beans/walnuts/green, leafy vegetables

3 Butter will burn when heated in a pan due to the milk solid molecules within the fat. The smoke point of butter is quite low meaning that it cannot reach high enough temperatures to crisp foods. An alternative is to use ghee, which is a butter with the milk solids removed.

4 The smoke point of a fat or oil is the temperature at which a blue smoke starts to be produced. The next stage is spontaneous ignition with the fat/oil on fire. Each fat or oil has a different smoke point.

5 fructose/glucose/galactose

6 sucrose/lactose/maltose

Notes: GB = Grade boost; QF = Quickfire; definitions can be found in the Glossary for all Grade boosts asking you to learn key words.

Principles of Nutrition (pages 6–17)

GB Macronutrients: protein, fat, carbohydrate; Micronutrients: vitamins and minerals

1,000 mg in 1g

QF1 Macronutrients are needed in large amounts each day, e.g. 50g protein, whereas micronutrients are needed in small amounts daily, e.g. vitamin C 30mg

GB 1g protein provides 4kcal energy; 1g carbohydrate provides 3.4kcal energy; 1g fat provides 9kcal energy

QF2 HBV: meat, milk, cheese, eggs, fish, soya; LBV: peas, beans, nuts, pulses, lentils

QF3 Children need ten essential amino acids.

QF4 Essential amino acids: valine, isoleucine, leucine, phenylalanine, threonine, tryptophan, methionine, lysine

QF5 Lentil soup with a bread roll, bean salad with rice, vegetable lasagne

QF6 1g protein = 4kcals

QF7 HBV proteins contain all the essential amino acids needed daily; LBV proteins lack one or more essential amino acids.

GB Fat is needed for warmth, organ protection and hormone production; the difference between saturated and unsaturated fat is that saturated fat is solid at room temperature.

QF9 See chart on page 12.

QF10 Hidden sugars are found in all processed or pre-made foods, e.g. tomato ketchup, baked beans. You can't see the sugar and it isn't always obvious that the food contains sugar.

QF11 It should contain wholemeal bread, rice or pasta plus vegetables and a piece of fruit.

QF12 Fibre in 100g fruit: blackcurrants 8g, blackberries 7g, raspberries 7g; fibre in 100g vegetable: leeks 24g, broad beans 7g, okra 7g

QF13 White bread 3g; granary bread 2.9g; wholemeal bread 9g

GB 1g carbohydrate gives 3.4kcals of energy; sugar carbohydrates are quickly absorbed into the blood causing unstable sugar levels; sugary carbohydrates, mouth bacteria and saliva mix to create an acidic medium which causes damage to tooth enamel resulting in decay and dental caries; Dietary fibre/NSP is vital to expel waste from the body, control blood sugar levels and reduce blood cholesterol.

QF14 Saturated: butter, lard, suet, ghee; monounsaturated: olive oil, sesame oil, peanut oil; polyunsaturated: sunflower oil, walnut oil, soybean oil

QF15 Fats and oils contain carbon, hydrogen and oxygen molecules. A double bond occurs when one or more carbon molecules joins to another carbon molecule. This prevents hydrogen from joining with that particular carbon molecule, preventing fat from becoming hard.

QF16 LDL is classed as a 'bad' fat, which can lead to heart disease, whereas HDL fat provides omega 3 and omega 6, which help reduce the risk of heart disease.

QF17 Beef topside, rib, sirloin; pork and lamb chops

QF18 Any named ready-made meal, mayonnaise, cakes, biscuits, crisps

GB 1g fat provides 9kcals; the difference between saturated and unsaturated fat is that saturated fat is solid at room temperature; LDL is classed as a 'bad' fat which can lead to heart disease, whereas HDL fats provide omega 3 and omega 6 which help reduce the risk of heart disease; fat in the bloodstream sticks to the inside of arteries which over time can cause a blockage. This will stop blood flowing, which may result in a stroke or a heart attack that can lead to disability or death.

QF19 Grill the bacon, sausages, tomatoes and mushrooms; poach or boil the eggs

QF20 Fruit: strawberries 77mg/100g, kiwi 59mg/100g; vegetables: red peppers 127mg/100g, kale 120mg/100

GB B group vitamins see chart on page 15; vitamin C per 100g fruit: kiwi, strawberries, oranges; vegetables: red peppers, kale, broccoli; vitamin D deficiency is caused because many people do not eat oily fish and liver, which are very good sources. Sunlight is a good way of obtaining vitamin D but many people do not expose their skin to the sun so they miss this excellent opportunity to access the vitamin. Expose skin daily for about 15–20 minutes – please don't allow your skin to burn.

QF21 Both conditions have weakened, soft bones. Osteomalacia occurs in adults, whereas rickets is a childhood condition.

QF22 Calcium: beans, broccoli, butternut squash, dried figs; iron: lentils, tofu, brown rice, cashew nuts

QF23 Bacon, soy sauce, tomatoes, stock cubes

QF24 The correct name for salt is sodium chloride. The sodium in sodium chloride is the health issue. 6g salt contains 2.4g sodium, making the RNI either 6g salt or 2.4g sodium.

QF25 Calcium + vitamin D: egg mayo sandwich plus milkshake, salmon in a cheese sauce; vitamin C + iron: bean and tomato salad, spinach and ricotta ravioli, sirloin steak with peas

GB Calcium: milk and cheese are good sources of calcium, which is needed for bone growth, and maintenance and nerve function. A lack of calcium results in soft, weak and fragile bones.

Iron: red meat, liver and dark green vegetables are good sources of iron, which is needed for the formation of haemoglobin. A lack of iron results in anaemia.

Sodium: cheese, tomatoes and salt are good sources of sodium, which is needed to maintain cell water levels and for nerves and muscles. Too much sodium can lead to high blood pressure and strokes.

Vitamin C works to improve iron absorption; vitamin D works to improve calcium absorption.

QF26 Iodine makes thyroid hormones and is found in shellfish, seaweed, dairy foods; zinc fights infections and heals skin, and is found in wholegrain cereals, dairy foods, meat; fluoride hardens tooth enamel and is found in kale, some drinking water and fish; selenium is an antioxidant which helps the immune system and is found in Brazil nuts, red meat, eggs.

Diet and Good Health (pages 20–22)

QF1a) 39%; **b)** 37%; **c)** 1%

QF2 Potatoes are vegetables but according to healthy eating are classed as a carbohydrate food.

QF3 If too much energy is taken in the body will gain weight. If too little energy is taken in the body will lose weight.

QF4 Kilocalorie (kcal) or kilojoule (kJ)

QF5 Weight gain, obesity, type 2 diabetes, cardiovascular disease

QF6 Cardiovascular disease, type 2 diabetes, anaemia, coeliac disease

GB A balanced diet is one that contains all the essential nutrients in the correct amounts. The diet must not have an excess or lack of any specific nutrient; fruit and vegetables 39% and starchy foods 37%; an allergy is an immune system reaction that can cause death; an intolerance is caused by a food that cannot be properly digested producing unpleasant symptoms.

QF7 Soya and soya products

QF8 Dried fruits, wholegrain cereals, dark green, leafy vegetables

The Science of Cooking Food (pages 26–30)

QF1 To make it safe to eat, to improve flavour and texture, to soften the food, to make it hot

QF2 Conduction, convection, radiation

QF3 a) Heat is transferred by direct contact of two surfaces, e.g. frying an egg; **b)** Heat is transferred by currents of hot air or liquid, e.g. boiling potatoes; **c)** Heat is transferred through waves of heat, e.g. grilling bacon.

QF4 Dry methods: roasting, grilling, baking, deep frying; moist methods: boiling, stewing, braising, steaming, poaching

GB Conduction heat is transferred by direct contact of two surfaces; convection heat is transferred by currents of hot air or liquid;

radiant heat is transferred through heat waves.

QF5 Protein molecular characteristics change. They becoming firm when heated, whisked or kneaded. Examples are frying an egg or making meringue.

QF6 Proteins change from a liquid state to a solid state. This is irreversible. Examples are scrambled egg and quiche.

QF7 The sugar melts caramelising the biscuit surface and on cooling creates the crisp texture. The flour coagulates creating the structure and dextrins are formed on the surface to create the nutty flavour.

QF8 At room temperature a fat is firm or solid and an oil is liquid.

QF9 The plasticity of fat in a cake mixture allows it to be beaten and still hold its 'mass', allowing the cake mix to be spreadable in the cake tin.

QF10 Answers can be found in the glossary.

GB Gelatinisation: roux, béchamel sauces.

QF11 Lemon juice tenderises meat by breaking down connective tissue making it softer to eat. Lemon juice added to egg white before whisking allows more air to be beaten and makes the foam stable. Casein in milk will start to clump together when lemon juice is added, especially if the milk is hot.

QF12 Marinades made with tomatoes, lemon juice and yoghurt create a flavoursome, acidic medium to soften the connective tissue of meat. The marinade adds flavour, moisture and tenderises meat.

QF13 Emulsion is where an oil and a watery liquid are held together in a suspension such as oil, egg yolk and vinegar mixed to form a mayonnaise.

QF14 Butter/margarine and egg

QF15 Any named cheese

QF16 Yeast

QF17 Bacteria

QF18 Choux buns, Yorkshire pudding, popovers, puff pastry, soufflé

QF19 a) Victoria sandwich, fairy cakes, scones, suet pastry; **b)** gingerbread, chocolate cake, scones; **c)** gingerbread, soda bread

QF20 Strong flour has strong gluten, which can really stretch and hold its shape. If 'ordinary' flour is used the gluten structure would collapse because it is not strong enough.

Food Spoilage (pages 35–39)

QF1 Bacteria that are harmful and cause food poisoning.

QF2 Campylobacter, Salmonella, Staph A, E. coli

QF3 Dirty hands touching food; using dirty equipment; poor personal hygiene; coughing; spitting; licking fingers; raw food touching cooked food

QF4 Answers can be found in the Glossary.

GB −18°C temperature at which frozen food is stored and bacteria cannot grow; 5°C is fridge storage temperature for chilled food. Bacteria still grow but slowly; 63°C is the lowest temperature for hot-held foods. Bacteria grow slowly at this temperature; 75°C is the minimum core temperature for cooked foods to be sure that most bacteria are killed.

Food waste must be reduced to prevent it going to landfill. Food waste can be reduced by only buying what is needed and using a shopping list that is devised after planning the week's meals. Use all leftovers the next day or freeze them for a future meal. Preventing food waste will also save the family money. Personal hygiene helps to prevent cross-contamination.

QF5 Warmth, food, time, oxygen, pH

QF6 Because bacteria will still grow in the fridge, although slowly.

QF7 Sugar, vinegar, lemon juice, tomatoes

QF8 Any dishes made from meat, fish, eggs, dairy. Dishes using stock and gravy. Dishes that won't be cooked, e.g. salads, cheesecake. Pasta and rice salads.

QF9 Campylobacter, raw poultry, meat, milk, sewage: abdominal pain, bloody diarrhoea, nausea, fever; Salmonella, gut of humans and animals: raw poultry: abdominal pain, diarrhoea, nausea, vomiting; Staph A., human skin, hair, nose, spots, cuts: abdominal pain and cramps, vomiting, chills; E. coli, human and animal sewage, muddy veg, raw meat: abdominal pain, diarrhoea, fever, vomiting, kidney damage

GB Campylobacter, Salmonella, Staph. A. and E. coli; −18°C temperature at which frozen food is stored and bacteria cannot grow; 5°C is fridge storage temperature for chilled food: bacteria still grow but slowly; 63°C is the lowest temperature for hot-held foods: bacteria grow slowly at this temperature; 75°C is the minimum core temperature for cooked foods to be sure that most bacteria are killed.

Dried food has had all the moisture removed; freezing creates a very cold, hostile environment; canning seals and heat treats food in cans or jars; pickling stores food in vinegar. All these methods prevent bacterial growth.

QF10 a) foods stored in vinegar so stop bacteria growing; **b)** foods stored at −18°C to prevent bacterial growth; **c)** foods are cooked and vacuum sealed in cans, giving a very long shelf life; **d)** the moisture is removed from food so bacteria can't grow, e.g. coffee and milk.

QF11 Biological: moulds, bacteria, yeasts; chemical: washing-up liquid, kitchen cleaners, air freshener, bleach; physical: jewellery, hair, nails, spit, nuts and bolts from machinery

QF12 Cross-contamination is the transfer of bacteria from one food to another or from humans, animals and equipment to food.

QF13

Packaging	Advantages	Disadvantages
Paper	Lightweight, can be printed on	Easily broken/torn
Card	Can have company logo on it; recyclable	Absorbs moisture; absorbs grease
Plastic	Lightweight, see-through; MAP; can be printed on; can be shaped to fit food	Some plastics not recyclable
Metal	Very strong; lightweight; long shelf life; recyclable	Not eco-friendly to make
Glass	Long shelf life; recyclable	Not eco-friendly to make; easily broken

QF14 It depends on your local authority but most paper, card, cans and glass can be recycled.

Food Provenance and Food Waste (pages 42–45)

QF1 Depends on area.

QF2 Depends on student's fridge.

QF3 The red tractor mark means that the food has been produced responsibly, from farm to fork, and is safe to eat.

QF4 Shoppers should buy seasonal local produce. Use local shops and walk don't drive.

QF5 a) breadcrumbs, puddings: summer, bread and butter, bread; **b)** fish cakes, duchess potatoes, in soup, pan fried; **c)** trifle, truffles, with custard; **d)** into a soup or casserole

QF6 It is a problem because it ends up in precious landfill sites and helps create greenhouse gases. It is a waste of money for families.

QF7 Recycled packaging will be used to make new packaging, whereas in a landfill it takes decades to break down. Paper and card will compost, whereas plastics do not degrade and are toxic to the land.

QF8 Paper, card, glass, cans

GB Ideal packaging materials include plastic, which is thin, light, can be moulded to the food's shape and is see-through; cardboard can have important information printed on it and can be recycled; foil is light, recyclable and can be shaped around food.

QF9 These foods have a shelf life of only up to five days and people often don't get around to eating them and before they know it the meal is out of date so it ends up being thrown into the bin. Also, people get confused between 'best before' and 'use by' dates, throwing the food away after the best before but before the use by date. Foods can be safely eaten after the best before date.

Cultures and Cuisines (pages 49–51)

QF1 a) oats, potatoes, wheat, raspberries, loganberries; **b)** wheat, maize, oats, apples, potatoes; **c)** wheat, olives, oranges, lemons, almonds, tomatoes, salad veg

QF2 Wheat, potatoes, sugar beet, oats, rapeseed oil

QF3 Lamb

GB Some crops prefer cold, wet areas like the Scottish hills and others need fairly dry, warm land to grow. For example, if wheat grows in very wet areas it has a higher chance of developing moulds and fungi. Strawberries grow in warm ground and need the sun to develop their sweet flavour.

QF4 There is a huge range of answers to this question. However, the answer cannot include any of the following: **a)** no pork or pork products and the meat must be halal; **b)** no pork or pork products and the foods must be kosher. Meat and milk must not be eaten in the same meal so a roast would not be served with either Yorkshire pudding or cauliflower cheese; **c)** eat a vegan diet so no animal or animal products to be included.

GB Kosher: foods prepared according to Jewish law. Ritual animal slaughter – death must be instant with no pain to the animal; Halal: foods prepared according to Islamic law. Animal are killed by slitting the throat.

QF5 People migrating to the UK bring with them their different cuisines and ingredients, which many people have adopted, e.g. curries, lasagne, lamb tagine.

QF6 The list is not exhaustive: **a)** tomatoes, mozzarella, parmesan, olives; **b)** wine, garlic, brie, mustard; **c)** olive oil, aubergine, goat, fish, olives, thyme; **d)** beef, sweetcorn, beans, clams; **e)** Serrano ham, chorizo, olive oil, rice; **f)** chick peas, dried fruits, fava beans, cinnamon, cumin; **g)** sticky and jasmine rice, tamarind paste, chillies, coconut milk, lemon grass, fish; **h)** sushi rice, soy sauce, fish, seaweed, rice vinegar; **i)** sweetcorn, beans, potatoes, pumpkin, cabbage

Technological Developments (pages 54–55)

QF1 & 2 Transport: how will the food be transported? Does it need cold storage? Preservation: is there a short shelf life? Does the food need preserving to make it last longer? Does the food need specific packaging, e.g. MAP to extend shelf life? Advertising: foods with added health benefits need advertising to inform customers.
Apps and barcodes: allow people to share product information. Barcodes allow traceability.
Environmental: can the packaging be recycled? Is the food organic/sustainable?
Science: companies are constantly researching and developing new ideas.
Money: all products must be cost effective and profit making.
Consumers: demand new products to fit their lifestyles and nutritional needs.
Robots: are reliable and cheaper than employing people. They work 24/7.
Lifestyle: people have more leisure time and money allowing them to buy pre-made foods.

GB Robots and automation have advanced food technology because factory lines can work 24/7 without needing breaks, becoming tired or making mistakes. This makes production faster and more profitable than employing people to do the same tasks. Scientific advances have helped

to increase shelf life of perishable foods. Environmental concerns have encouraged food manufacturers to produce foods in a more environmentally friendly way. Functional foods are those that have additional characteristics such as boosting health benefits or reducing the risk of disease.
Fairtrade is a system where developing world farmers are fairly paid for the crops they grow.

QF3 Answers can be found in the Glossary.

QF4 The Eatwell Guide is a visual aid to help people eat a healthy, balanced diet by illustrating how much fruit/vegetables, carbohydrates and protein to eat. It recommends eating minimal fat and sugary foods.

QF5 The Change4Life initiative encourages people to maintain a healthy weight and include exercise in their daily lives.

Factors Affecting Food Choice (pages 59–63)

QF1 a) June–August; **b)** July–October; **c)** November–March; **d)** September–March; **e)** September–March; **f)** August–October

QF2 Costs are approximate and will change/vary: **a)** chick peas 20p; **b)** lentils 23p; **c)** minced beef 80p; **d)** canned tuna 70p

GB a) no particular dietary rules; **b)** do not eat any meat and do not drink alcohol; **c)** follow a lacto-vegetarian diet and regularly fast; **d)** do not eat meat, shellfish or salt

QF3 Organic food is made from crops and livestock that have not been sprayed with or eaten chemical pesticides and fertilisers.

QF4 Farm Assured promotes and regulates food quality. Fairtrade is a system whereby farmers from the developing world are paid a fair sum for they crops and labour.

QF5 Peanuts, nuts, wheat, milk, shellfish, oranges, strawberries, eggs

QF6 Lactose intolerance

GB Factors that influence what we buy include: what the family has always purchased; price and offers; advertising; social media; placement in the supermarket; children's pester power
New products are brought to market after extensive research, development, trialling and customer feedback. An idea is developed, with market research carried out. The product is then refined and improved depending on customer feedback before going into mass production. If, at any stage, there are serious problems the product may be cancelled so the company does not make too great a financial loss.
To reduce carbon footprints: where possible, buy foods in bulk once a month, take the bus or walk to the shops, only buy what is actually needed, use bags for life, have the shopping delivered, buy local produce.

QF7 Primary research is collecting information and data using surveys and questionnaires; secondary research is collecting information that other people may have already collected, e.g. information

from websites, magazines; product placement is where products are placed at eye level in a supermarket or clearly seen in a film or TV programme.

QF8 Pester power is when children pester parents to buy specific products that parents wouldn't ordinarily buy.

GB Read and learn what information is on food labels.

QF9 Blind testing: consumer cannot see what they are testing so they cannot be influenced; ranking test: consumers rank the product from best to worst; rating test: consumers rate each product 1–5.

Basic Mixtures and Recipes (pages 67–73)

GB Think about these points.

QF1 a) ½ fat to flour; **b)** ¾ fat to flour

QF2 Approximately 65°C

QF3 Cornflour is made from maize, contains no glutenin/gliadin proteins and cannot 'rise', whereas plain flour is made from wheat and does contain these proteins.

QF4 Tough cuts of beef that need plenty of cooking: shin, stewing, chuck, brisket, braising

QF5 Chopped parsley, lemon wedges, slices of tomatoes, dill

QF6 Feather, buttercream, fudge, royal, fondant, glacé

QF7 Whisking method

QF8 Coffee gateau: coffee buttercream whirls and walnuts; summer fruit roulade: whirls of whipped cream and strawberries

QF9 A standard bread dough is made from flour, water, a little margarine and yeast; a rich bread dough includes egg, milk, butter and sometimes sugar.

QF10 Both are strips of carrot. Batons are chunkier than the thin julienne strips.

QF11 Foam

QF12 Gelatine

QF13 Bring the liquid ingredients to the boil and continue boiling until much of the liquid had evaporated, leaving a syrupy sauce.

QF14 Creaming or all-in-one method

QF15 Because the sugar in the cooked mixture is hot. Once the biscuits cool the sugar hardens creating a crisp biscuit.

QF16 Warmth, moisture, food, oxygen and time

QF17 Flour, sugar and margarine or butter. Oats, dried fruit and nuts can also be added.

QF18 White, granary, 50/50, wheatmeal, wholegrain, seeded or wholemeal bread; ciabatta, brioche, sour dough, soda breads

QF19 Green salad, coleslaw, rice salad, chips

QF20 Basil

QF21 Equal quantities: fat, sugar, flour and eggs should all weigh the same.

Cereals (pages 74–81)

QF1 a) Cereals are good staple foods in the developing world because they are a good source of nutrients, cheap to produce, can be stored for a long time and each hectare of land produces more kg of food than if the same land was used for animal production; **b)** Cereals are stocked in all supermarkets and are cheap to buy compared to meat and fish.

QF2 Check your answer in the textbook.

QF3 Pies, cakes, bread, biscuits

QF4 The wheat grains have to be very finely crushed to break the hard bran surface. The inside of the grain is called endosperm and is ground to form flour. To make bread, mix the flour with yeast and water to form an elastic dough. The dough must be kneaded to work the gluten (protein) in the wheat. The dough is left to prove /rise before being shaped and cooked.

QF5 Wheat, rye, barley, rice, oats, maize

QF6 Store in an airtight container in a cupboard.

QF7 a) Contains a strong mix of proteins allowing bread to rise; **b)** given time and warmth produces CO_2 bubbles to raise the dough; **c)** brings all the dry ingredients together to form a dough; **d)** add flavour, helps gluten to form and controls the rate of CO_2 production.

QF8 Warmth, moisture, food, time, oxygen

QF9 a) Mixing, kneading, proving, knocking back, shaping, proving and baking; **b)** bread is made much more quickly than the traditional method, which allows the factory to produce more loaves in 24 hours. More sales equals more income.

QF10 They are unleavened so have a very different texture from bread. They are unleavened so have a very different texture from bread, e.g. tortilla wraps are thin and pliable, allowing them to be wrapped around food.

QF11 The larger and chunkier the pasta shape the thicker the sauce needs to be. Thin strands of pasta should be served with light, creamy sauces, e.g. pasta shells and penne with thick meaty or vegetable sauces and spaghetti or linguine with thin creamy or tomato sauces.

QF These details can all be found in the textbook.

QF12 a) Al dente means with bite. Pasta should be firm and not soft to the bite; **b)** wholemeal pasta contains more fibre and keeps you feeling fuller for longer.

GB Bacterial spores are formed in unfavourable conditions such as excessive heat. The bacteria can develop thick outer cell walls allowing the bacteria to remain dormant for a long time.

Salmonella-free eggs are stamped with a lion or dragon mark. This certifies that they are from salmonella-free hens.

GB During digestion, soluble fibre is absorbed, keeps us feeling fuller longer and helps to reduce blood cholesterol. Insoluble fibre cannot be absorbed, so passes through the body fairly unchanged, helping to prevent constipation.

Fruit and Vegetables (pages 84–91)

QF1 Root: carrot, parsnip, swede, celeriac, turnip, beetroot; stem: celery, globe artichoke, asparagus, rhubarb, endive; pods: runner beans, peas, sweetcorn, sugarsnap peas, lentils, pomegranate; leaf: cabbage, lettuce, spinach, watercress; flower: broccoli, cauliflower, berries, apples, pears, citrus

QF2 Hard: apples, pears; soft: all berries; citrus: oranges, limes, lemons, grapefruit; tropical: lychee, mango, jack fruit, guava, pineapple; dried: sultanas, raisins, dates, figs, apricots; stoned: plum, peach, nectarine, apricot

QF3 Apricots, passion fruit, papaya, water melon

QF4 Potatoes, carrots, swede, sweetcorn, parsnips

QF5 Because the skin adds fibre and micro-nutrients to the meal. Peeled potatoes lose these benefits.

QF6 September–March

QF7 Oxygen

QF8 Soak them in a pan of cold water.

GB Answers are in the text.

QF9 Firm, good red colour, no bruising or splits to skin, smell fresh

QF10 Plastic bags create humidity, which is not an ideal environment, causing spoilage to speed up.

GB Canning: vegetables are blanched to kill surface bacteria. Cans or jars must be sterilised in boiling water. Vegetables and slightly salted water are placed in the can or jar. The jars or cans are sealed and placed in a water bath or pressure cooker and heated to a temperature to kill harmful bacteria. On cooling, a vacuum seal forms which stops air getting into the foods.

Green, leafy veg can be packed in MAP packaging because the mix of gases in the sealed package will prevent them from oxidising, which maintains the colour and extends the shelf life.

QF11 Prepare just before cooking. Wash the leaves in cold water – do not soak them. Shred the leaves into thin slices and cook immediately to prevent vitamin loss.

QF12 Wash the strawberries under cold water. Remove the green calyx and cut the strawberries into thick slices or quarters.

QF13 Cut the apples into quarters, remove core and thinly peel each piece. Place into a bowl of cold water + lemon juice to prevent browning. Cut each ¼ into slices and place back in the lemon water until required.

QF14 Potatoes, swede, turnip, artichokes, parsnips, runner beans, broccoli, greens, sprouts

QF15 Cabbage, onions, kale, spinach

QF16 Potatoes, sprouts, onions, carrots, greens, asparagus, leeks

QF17 a) March–July Strawberries **b)** June–August; **c)** October–April; **d)** April–June; **e)** September–April; **f)** October–February

Milk, Cheese and Yoghurt (pages 98–106)

QF1 Harmful

QF2 Listeria, tuberculin, E. coli

QF3 a) blue; **b)** green; **c)** red

QF4 Old milk has more bacteria in than new milk and by mixing them together the new milk will become more contaminated and will not last as long as it should.

QF5 Sunlight can cause milk to develop an 'off' flavour and the B vitamins are destroyed by sunlight.

QF6 To kill any harmful/pathogenic bacteria.

QF7 Listeria, tuberculin and E. coli

QF8 Pasteurised milk is forced through very fine mesh to break up the fat (cream) globules.

QF9 For growth, repair and cell maintenance

QF10 For bone growth and development, nerve function and blood clotting

QF11 Rickets in children and osteomalacia in adults

GB Pasteurisation: milk is heated to 75°C for 25 seconds; homogenisation: milk is forced through fine meshes to break down large fat globules into smaller ones, so that the cream is evenly dispersed.

The fat from skimmed milk is dried and incorporated into ready-made products.

Milk goes off if the bottle is not closed, left in a warm room, in the sunlight or mixed with older milk.

QF12 There are numerous dishes.

QF13 a) 100ml soya milk = 25mg; **b)** 100ml almond milk = 1mg; **c)** 100ml rice milk = >1mg; however, most products are fortified with added calcium.

QF14 Lactose is the sugar found in milk, made from glucose and galactose.

QF15 Some people cannot digest lactose. It can cause flatulence and diarrhoea.

QF16 The milk needs to become semi-solid to be able to form into cheese.

QF17 Whey is the liquid part of milk once curds have formed.

QF18 Curds are the solid part of coagulated milk.

QF19 The blue mould spores are introduced to firm cheese via steel probes.

QF20 There are numerous answers to this.

QF21 Au gratin

QF22 High biological value

QF23 Feta, mozzarella, ricotta, cottage, quark

QF24 a) in drinks, poured on desserts, in a quiche; **b)** on fruit salad, on fruit pies; **c)** on fruit pies, in mousses, piped on cakes; **d)** double quenelles on desserts, in panna cotta, piped on cakes and desserts; **e)** clotted quenelles on desserts and scones

Meat, Poultry, Fish and Eggs (pages 113–121)

QF1 **a)** Beef, lamb, pork, venison, goat; **b)** chicken, turkey, duck, pheasant, goose; **c)** salmon, trout, mackerel, tuna, sardines, herring; **d)** cod, haddock, plaice, hake, coley; **e)** crab, prawns, lobster, crayfish

QF2 Beef: sirloin, brisket, rump, shin, rib, chuck, topside; pork: shoulder, loin, tenderloin, belly, cheek, leg, hock

QF3 Sardines, mackerel, trout, whitebait, lemon sole, sprats

GB Red meat has a fibrous texture due to the strands of muscle fibres. Marbling of white fat may be throughout the meat. Offal has a close, smooth texture, is very tender and cooks very quickly.

The fat found in oily fish is dispersed throughout the flesh causing it to be coloured. The fat in a white fish is found only in the liver which leaves the flesh white.

QF4 **a)** in a sealed container or deep tray at the bottom of the fridge or in the freezer; **b)** in a sealed container or freezer bag in the fridge, bottom shelf, or in the freezer**; c)** in a dish, covered with clingfilm, on the top shelf of the fridge

QF5 Campylobacter, salmonella, E. coli

QF6 **a)** Denaturing protein is altering the protein characteristics irreversibly through heat or mechanical action; **b)** cooked steak, fried egg, whisked egg white

QF7 It adds a brown colour, and gives a crispy texture and roasted meat flavour.

QF8 Tryptophan, lysine, leucine, isoleucine, histidine, methionine, phenylalanine, threonine, valine

QF9 Lean meat has very little visible fat.

QF10 White fish has no fat in the flesh and omega 3 is found in some fats. No fat = no omega 3

QF11 Too much saturated fat eaten regularly can result in blocked arteries leading to cardiovascular disease.

QF12 To tenderise meat marinade it in tomatoes/yoghurt, cut it into small pieces, bash it out, cook long and slow

QF13 Beef: shin, chuck, stewing, braising steak; lamb: breast, shin, neck

QF14 Beef: sirloin, rump, fillet; lamb: loin chops, best end, rack, top leg

QF15 Tough cuts are used in any named casseroles, stews or pot roasts.

QF16 Turkey, pheasant, emu, ostrich, guinea fowl

QF17 Battery: hens are kept in indoor cages where light, temperature and feed are controlled. This is the cheapest method of egg production; barn: like the battery method but the hens are not caged; free range: hens roam in the open air and are locked in hen houses at night; organic: hens live on spacious organic land and have organic feed. This is the most expensive method of egg production.

QF18 The lion/dragon mark means the eggs are salmonella free.

QF19 Yolk is the oily, protein rich part; albumen is the 'white' consisting of a thin white and a thick white. This is the 'watery' part; chalazae are the strands that hold the yolk in the white; air sac grows larger as the egg ages; shell membranes keep the egg fresh by filtering air getting into the egg; shell prevent damage to the egg and is porous.

GB Albumen

QF20 Aeration: air is trapped during whisking, which gives a light, airy texture to foods; binding: ingredients are 'glued' together with beaten egg which coagulates on heating; coating: beaten egg will stick breadcrumbs to food and goes crispy when cooked; glazing: beaten egg gives a golden shine to baked foods; emulsifying: egg yolk will enable oil and vinegar to stay in a stable emulsion; thickening: when heated egg will thicken a liquid, such as milk; enriching: eggs are very nutritious so adding eggs to a dish adds nutrients; garnish: sliced boiled egg adds colour to savoury dishes.

QF21 **a)** 60°C; **b)** 65°C–70°C

QF22 The answers are on page 121.

Beans, Nuts, Seeds, Soya, Tofu and Mycoprotein (pages 126–129)

QF1 Beans: haricot, aduki, lima, pinto, kidney, fava, black-eye, broad beans; lentils: red, brown, green, yellow, puy; peas: green peas, mange tout, sugarsnap peas; nuts: almonds, Brazil, hazelnuts, cashew, macadamia, pistachio

QF2 Beans are pod-borne seeds that provide fibre and LBV. Peas are usually green seeds but in some types the whole pod is eaten, e.g. mange tout. Lentils are small seeds grown in pods and are used for soups and in salads.

QF3 Dried kidney beans must be boiled for at least ten minutes to destroy a naturally occurring toxin.

QF4 Bean/lentil chilli, nut/lentil roast, bean/nut burger, puy lentil and nut salad

QF5 Pumpkin seeds are very nutritious containing good levels of fibre, iron, potassium and anti-oxidants. They are good for you, whereas sweets have very little nutrition and lots of calories, and contribute to tooth decay.

QF6 Lysine

GB Growth

QF7 Smoothies, frittatas, scrambled tofu, stir-fries, in soups, in crumbs and baked

QF8 Textured vegetable protein (see the textbook)

QF9 High biological value

QF10 Alternative proteins are low in fat so will not contribute to coronary vascular disease. Soya and quinoa are both HBV proteins providing all the essential amino acids required. Most alternative proteins are good sources of calcium.

GB High biological value

Butter, Oil, Margarine, Sugar and Syrup (pages 133–138)

QF1 Butter: cakes, pastry, biscuits; lard: pastry, roasting, frying; suet: pastry, steamed puddings; margarine: cakes, pastry, biscuits; Trex/Cookeen: pastry, roasting, frying

QF2 Fillet steak 8g; chicken breast 4g; loin venison 3g.

QF3 **a)** 100g crisps 35g; **b)** 100g chips 15g; **c)** 100g carrots 0.2g; **d)** 100g apples 0.2g

QF4 Omega 3 is found in flaxseed oils, fish oils, soya spread, rapeseed oil; omega 6 is found in grapeseed oil, sunflower oil and spread, corn oil, soyabean oil

QF5 Saturated: butter, ghee, lard, suet; monounsaturated: olive oil, rapeseed oil; polyunsaturated: sunflower oil, corn oil, soya oil

QF6 Butter 177°C; sunflower oil 227°C

QF Answers can be found in this book.

QF LDL and HDL are both discussed in this book.

QF7 Fat with extra hydrogen bonds plus anti-oxidants will extend shelf life because the fats take longer to go rancid and reduce the need for water-based moisture, resulting in a slower bacterial growth rate.

QF8 Lard or Trex

QF9 19kcals in 1 tsp sugar (5g)

QF10 Sugar beet

QF11 Vegans believe that all honey belongs to bees for their health and that humans eating honey is exploitation of bees.

GB Monosaccharide: honey, fruit and milk sugars; disaccharide : sugars used in drinks and cooking, maltose

QF12 Sugar is classed as empty calories because the sugar carbohydrate calories are not supported by any other nutrients. There is no good nutrition in sugar.

GLOSSARY

Advertising providing information to consumers about a product or service.

Aeration air is incorporated into food by sieving, creaming, whisking, beating, rubbing in or folding and rolling.

Al dente cooked until firm to the bite.

Albumen thick and thin, water-based egg white.

Allergen substance that can cause an allergic reaction.

Allergy an immune system reaction that occurs soon after eating a certain food.

Ambient foods food that can be stored, at room temperature, in a sealed container. All foods found on supermarket shelves are ambient foods.

Amino acid simpler unit of protein, made up of long chains.

Anaemia a condition where the body lacks enough healthy red blood cells or haemoglobin.

Anti-oxidant a molecule that is able to stop the oxidation process in other molecules and therefore can be useful in stopping foods from deteriorating. Anti-oxidants can prevent or slow down damage to our body, which otherwise can lead to diseases such as heart disease and cancers. Anti-oxidants also improve our immune system.

Applications (apps) self-contained programs or pieces of software designed to fulfil a particular purpose, especially as downloaded by a user to a mobile device.

Bacillus cereus a type of pathogenic bacteria that produces toxins, associated with poor hygiene, in cooked rice.

Bacteria single celled microorganisms.

Barn eggs eggs from chickens raised in a barn.

Binary fission the reproduction of one cell, splitting into two generically identical cells.

Biodegradable decomposesd by bacteria or other living organisms.

Bran the fragments of grain husk that are separated from flour after milling. When bran is removed from grains, there is a reduction in nutritional value. Bran can be milled from any cereal grain and can be found, for example, in rice, wheat, barley and corn.

Calcium deficiency also known as hypocalcaemia, where the body suffers from not having enough calcium for its needs.

Campylobacter pathogenic bacterium causing food poisoning.

Caramelise sugar/natural sugar becomes golden brown when heated.

Carbon footprint a carbon footprint measures the total carbon dioxide emissions caused directly and indirectly by a person, organisation, event or product.

Chilled food food stored between 1°C and 5°C.

Climate the weather conditions typical to an area in general or at any specific time.

Coagulate to become solid or to set.

Coeliac a person who suffers from a chronic intestinal disorder caused by sensitivity to the protein gliadin contained in the gluten of cereals.

Collagen protein in the connective tissue, which holds cells together.

Conduction heat from one surface is passed directly to another.

Convection heat is transferred to food through the circulation of liquid or gas molecules.

Convenience foods foods that need little preparation, especially foods that have been pre-prepared and preserved for long-term storage.

Core temperature the temperature of any food at its core – right in the centre.

Cross-contamination the transfer of bacteria from one food to another, from humans, animals, other food or equipment.

Cuisines styles of cooking.

Culture the way of life, and the general customs and beliefs of a particular group of people at a particular time.

Curds soft, white milk solids that form the basis of cheese.

Deficiency a state of lacking or incompleteness. For example, deficiencies in the consumption of certain vitamins can cause health issues.

Dehydration when water is lost or removed. For the body, losing too much water can be very dangerous to health and ultimately fatal.

Denature changes to proteins due to heat, acid, mechanical action or enzymes.

Dextrins a fibre in wheat that slows down digestion.

Diabetics people who suffer from diabetes, a condition that occurs when the body can't use glucose normally.

Disaccharides a carbohydrate made from two sugar molecules ('di' means two).

Double bond a chemical bond between two elements.

E. coli bacteria that can cause sickness, diarrhoea and fever.

Eatwell Guide a guide to healthy eating produced by the government.

Eight top tips a guide to healthy eating.

Emulsion an oil and water mixture, e.g. milk, mayonnaise.

Endosperm the main part of the grain, a starch and protein supply.

Environment our surroundings.

Enzymes biological catalysts that speed up biochemical reactions without being used up themselves. Digestive enzymes are important for the process of breaking down food so that the body can absorb nutrients from it.

Enzymic browning discolouration of certain foods caused by oxygen and enzymes.

Fairtrade a partnership between producers and consumers; selling on Fairtrade terms provides farmers with a better deal and more income. This allows them the opportunity to improve their lives and plan for their future.

Fortified when a nutrient is added to a food to increase its nutritional value.

Free range a method of farming, where, for at least part of the day, animals can roam freely outdoors.

Frozen food food that has been frozen rapidly and kept frozen until used.

Functional foods foods that have a positive effect beyond basic nutrition, such as boosting optimal health or reducing the risk of disease.

Gelatine the thickening of a mixture, in the presence of heat, due to the swelling of starch grains.

Genetically engineered food food that has had its DNA changed using genes from other plants.

Genetically modified (GM) food derived from organisms whose genetic material has been modified.

Germ a source of fat and B vitamins, it is where the new plant grows.

Glucose monosaccharide or simple sugar, found in fruit and vegetables.

Gluten formed from the two wheat proteins gliadin and gluterin, in the presence of water. Gluten is developed by kneading.

Greenhouse gases trap heat in the atmosphere so the Earth warms up.

Heat transference how heat moves from one area to another.

High density lipoprotein (HDL) cholesterol good blood cholesterol.

High pressure processing (HPP) a processing method that subjects food to elevated pressures (with or without the addition of heat) to render bacteria inactive.

High-risk foods foods that are easily contaminated by bacteria, for example shellfish.

Homogenisation in milk – large fat globules are broken down into smaller fat globules.

Hot-held foods cooked foods must be kept 63°C or above on hot-food counters.

Hydrogenated liquid fat or oil that has been changed to a solid, at room temperature, by the addition of hydrogen.

Hydroponic plants grown in a water-based environment rather than soil, e.g. tomatoes.

Insects any small arthropod animals that have six legs and generally one or two pairs of wings.

Insoluble fibre fibre that the body cannot absorb.

Insulin a hormone that controls blood sugar levels.

Intolerances when individual elements of certain foods cannot be properly processed and absorbed by the digestive system.

Kwashiorkor a form of malnutrition linked to protein deficiency.

Lacto vegetarians eat dairy foods but not eggs, milk or fish.

Lacto-ovo vegetarians eat dairy foods and eggs but not meat or fish.

Leavened bread made with a raising agent, such as yeast, so that it rises.

Legume upright or climbing bean or plant.

Locally your local area.

Low density lipoprotein (LDL) cholesterol bad blood cholesterol.

Macronutrients a class of chemical compounds that humans consume in the largest quantities.

Maillard reaction a chemical reaction between a protein and a carbohydrate in the presence of dry heat.

Market research the gathering and studying of data relating to consumer opinions and preferences, purchasing power, etc., especially prior to introducing a product to the market.

Marketing the activities involved in encouraging consumers to buy a product or service.

Micronutrients nutrients required in small quantities to facilitate a range of physiological functions.

Microorganisms usually single cell microscopic organisms such as bacteria, moulds and fungi.

Migration when people or animals move from one geographical area to another.

Milled the process of making wheat into flour.

Mirepoix mixture of small-diced foods.

Modified atmosphere packaging (MAP) food packaging that changes the internal atmosphere of the packet, normally reducing the amount of oxygen present to slow down food decay.

Monosaccharides simple carbohydrates (mono means one; saccharide means sugar).

Monounsaturated fat fat that contains one double bond in the molecule. This fat is associated with keeping cholesterol levels low. Examples of foods containing monounsaturated fat include red meats and avocados.

Moulds fungi that grow in filaments, creating a fuzzy appearance on food. They are soft, green or grey growths that develop on old food.

Mould spores a form of fungi used to colour and flavour cheese.

Mycoprotein a food made from the fungi family that contains all the essential amino acids needed by the body. Suitable for lacto-ovo vegetarians.

Myoglobin a protein that stores oxygen in the muscle cells of animals.

New foods foods where the nutrition h as been modified or enhanced.

Nutrients the properties found in food and drinks that give the nourishment vital for growth and the maintenance of life. The main nutrients needed by the human body are carbohydrates, proteins, fats, vitamins and minerals.

Oedema fluid retention in the body, which often causes feet and ankles to swell.

Organic any food that is grown or made without the use of chemicals.

Organic eggs eggs from chickens that are not fed with any chemicals.

Origin the place from which something is derived.

Osteomalacia a softening of the bones, through deficiency of calcium or vitamin D.

Osteoporosis a medical condition in which the bones become brittle and fragile.

Oxidising of enzymes enzymes affected by oxygen.

Pathogenic causes disease.

Pathogenic bacteria harmful bacteria.

Pellagra a deficiency disease due to a lack of vitamin B3 (niacin) in the diet. Causes skin, nerve and mental health problems plus diarrhoea. Often occurs where maize is a staple food.

Perishable foods foods that will decay or go 'bad' quickly.

Pester power the ability of a child to nag a parent relentlessly until the parent succumbs and agrees to purchase something they would not normally buy.

pH value how acid or alkaline a food is.

Plasticity fat softness or spreadability.

Polyunsaturated fat fat that contains several double or even triple bonds in the molecule. Examples of foods that contain polyunsaturated fats include salmon, flaxseeds and walnuts.

Preservation/preserve keeping something in its present state or preventing it from being damaged.

Primary processing the conversion of raw materials into food commodities, for example milling of wheat grain into flour.

Probiotic a microorganism that, when taken in adequate amounts,. confers a health benefit.

Product placement placing a product in a prominent position to encourage people to buy it.

Quick response codes (QR codes) a two-dimensional barcode that can be read by smartphones and links directly to text, emails, websites or phone numbers.

Radiation transfer of heat through particles or waves, e.g. grilling.

Rancid unpleasant smell or flavour in fats and meat.

Reference nutrient intake (RNI) an estimate of the amount of proteins, vitamins and minerals that should meet the needs of most of the group to which they apply.

Rickets a health condition when the bones become soft due to a lack of vitamin D or calcium.

Salmonella pathogenic bacteria found in raw eggs.

Saturated fat fat in which all of the carbon atoms in the fatty acid molecules are linked by single bonds. This type of fat is mostly from animal sources and can be bad for our health.

Secondary processing converting primary processed foods into other food products, for example flour into biscuits.

Shortening butter, lard or other fat that remains solid at room temperature, used for making pastry or bread.

Soluble fibre fibre that attracts and dissolves in water, so is easier to digest than insoluble fibre but still slows and improves the digestion process. Examples of foods that contain high proportions of soluble fibre include barley, beans, nuts, seeds, lentils, peas, and some fruit and vegetables.

Staple food food that forms a large part of the diet, usually from starchy foods.

Starch a polysaccharide, a complex carbohydrate.

Starchy carbohydrate a polysaccharide/complex carbohydrate, as in bread, pasta, potatoes and beans.

Strong flour flour with a higher gluten content, e.g. bread flour.

Sugar a monosaccharide or disaccharide, a simple carbohydrate.

Sustainable a human activity that is not harmful to the environment and does not deplete natural resources, thereby supporting long-term ecological balance.

Syneresis the sudden release of moisture from protein molecules.

Traceability the ability to track any food through all stages of production, processing and distribution.

Traditions customs, ways of living or beliefs that are recognised as very long established and typically passed from one generation to another over time.

Ultra-heat treatment (UHT) heat treatment of liquids to 135°C for 1–2 seconds.

Unleavened bread bread made not using a raising agent so it does not rise.

Unsaturated fats fats that contain a high ratio of fatty acid molecules with at least one double bond. Unsaturated fats are considered to be the healthier than saturated fats. Examples of foods containing unsaturated fats include rape seed oil and olive oil.

Whey the watery part of soured milk.

Vegan a person who does not use or eat any animal products, such as leather, meat or dairy.

Wholegrains 100% of the grains, nothing has been removed.

Yeasts microorganisms belonging to the fungi family, made up of single oval cells that reproduce by budding. Yeasts can ferment sugar into alcohol and carbon dioxide, and are also used as a raising agent when making bread.

INDEX

Photo acknowledgements

p4 Dragon Images; p6 bitt24; baibaz; p7 Africa Studio; Velychko Viktoriia; margouillat photo; marekuliasz; haveseen; maradon 333; p8 Medicshots / Alamy Stock Photo; alexpro9500; p10 Sszekeres Szabiocs; p11 Brian Yarvin; Ari N; p12 DUSAN ZIDAR; Africa Studio; solara22; p13 Diana Talium; Sea Wave; Valtyn Volkov; Nata-Lia; hywoods; p14Maks Narodenko; WEB-DESIGN; saschanti 17; iprachenko; p15 saschanti17; Anna Mente; Bogdan Wankowicz; p16 hiphoto; etorres; p17 Paul Brady Photo; Mamsizz; Tarasyuk Igor; p19 Viktor1; p21 Timmary; Pablo Prat; p20 Crown copyright; Juice Team; p21 Artgraphixel; p21 Anna.zabella; Tefi; joshya; Hong Vo; p22 Aleksandar Mijatovic; p23 rweisswald; p24 Juice Team; p26 GreenArt; p27 MiIGUEL GARCIA SAAVEDRA; MicO_J; Africa Studio; Andrey Armyagov; Douglas Freer; p28 AlenaKogotkova; Monkey Business Images; Moving Moment; Jiri Hera; Jayne Hill; Ari N; p29 Igor Vkv; Jayne Hill; Valentyn Volkov; Ivasschenko Roman; Tobik; aquariagirl1970; p30 Domenic Gareri; thefoodphotographer; Chalermsak; p31 GreenArt; stocksolutions; Richard M Lee; Zero99; p33 margouillat photo; p32 Lestertair; p34 O'SHI; p35 tatui suwat; Africa Studio; p38 Svetlana Foote; p39 Lyudmila Suvorova; Fotofermer; Photosiber; Oxana Denezhkina; Luisa Leal Photography; p40 GMEVIPHOTO; AS Food studio; p42 Jess Wealleans; Christian Mueller / Shutterstock.com; p44 Sakonboon Sansri; Tobik; NokHoOkNoi; witoon214; Air Images; Baloncici; p45 AdamBoor; banksy_boy; Nick Stubbs; Joe Gough; Billion Photos; jennyt; gabriel12; p46 Gts; p51 Ttally / Shutterstock, Inc.; 1989studio; p48 Viktoria Roy; 48 beboy; Curioso; p49 Stockr; p50 Leonid S. Shtandel; umiko; p52 vectorfusionart; Thinglass / Shutterstock, Inc.; p53 Robert Kneschke; Fairtrade Austria; Assured Food Standards; Soil Association; p54 Xinhua / Alamy Stock Photo; p55 gooffygolf; David Crockett; Xinhua; p56 Fairtrade Austria; Assured Food Standards Association; muph; p58 Marukosu; littleny; p59 wldenstroem; Roman Samokhin; photogal; Andrey Eremin; Tim UR; Y Photo Studio; waldenstroen; Somachai Som; Binh Thanh Bui; kaiskynet; kaiskynet; greatstockimages; p60 Africa Studio; Ekaterina_ Minaeava; Gunnerl; p61 Fairtrade Austria; Assured Food Standards; Graphic Compressor; THPStock; p62 Mar Photographics / Alamy Stock Photo; p63 Courtesy of Tesco; p64 Ditty_about_summer; p66 Golubovy; p67 studiostoks; Maly Designer; p68 D Pimborough; EQRoy; margouillat photo; stocksoultions; Emiel de Lange; 5 Second Studio; seeshooteatrepeat; siamionau pavel; p69 ScriptX; shutterdandan; Freedom_Studio; Elena Veselova; bioraven; Alex Tihonovs; Ozgur Coskun; Kondor83; p70 Africa Studio; Moving Moment; stockcreations; Anna Shepulova; PiraPora; p71 indigolotos; Elena Demyanko; Gitanna; Felix Furo; Natatika; Diana Taliun; p72 Tatiana Volgutova; topnatthapon; Civil; p73 stocksoultions; Jasmine_K; Koto Moto; p74 Texturis; leonori; focal point; Brent Hofacker; perfectlab; id-art; p75 jabiru; p76 Scorpp; p77 Africa Studio; Mita Stock Images; p78 Africa Studio; kuvona; p79 Sony Ho; p80 Ed Samuel; inlovepai; p81 Auhustsinovich; inlovepai; Brent Hofacker; Madlen; Sascha Burkard; JIB Liverpool; JoeyPhoto; Igor Grochev; COLOA Studio; Madlen; p82 Gita Kulinitch Studio; p83 AS Food studio; p84 montifcello; p85 Lepas; Danil Snigirev; IrinaK; Anna Kucherova; Elena Schweltzer; p86 Nattika; d1SK; Lotus Images; SuperBelka; Ogdesign; Arcady; Binh Thanh Bui; Aurora72; Crown copyright; p87 Sebastian Studio; Jayne Hill; leonori; p88 Africa Studio; Billion Photos; Gts; posteriori; Anke van Wyk; Francesco83; p89 Warut Chinsai; Nogwish; qingqing; Englightened Media; Lotus Images; Lana Langlois; Peter Zijistra; p90 Richard Griffin; kazoka; Rogers S G Neves; Nitr; Lesterair; Shebeko; Leszek Glasner; p91 Christopher Elwell; Yala; p92 merc+7; FotoSajewicz; p93 Elena Veselova; p95 Kzenon; p96 Africa Studio; smereka; p97 symbiot; p98 Peter Zvonar; p99 imagedb; Carla Castro; p101 Olga Popova; wsf-s; Africa Studio; Tanya Sid: picturepartners; fotogiunta; vetassster; margouillat photo; Alasdair James; Hue Ta; Joe Gough; Tanya Sid; p102 ChiccoDodiFC; Paul Cowan; p103 Brent Hofacker; THANAN KONGDOUNG; Joshua Resnick; p104 AlexeyIvanov; p106 Paul Cowan; Viktor1; p108 Corepics VOF; p110 Phototasty; p111 veleknez; Tsekhmister; DenisNata; cynoclub; chris2766; weter 777; Richard Peterson; Coffeemill; p112 alain wacquier; n7atal7i; Alexandra Thompson; Oleksandr Lysenko; casanisa; bonchan; Angel Simon; bonchan; p116 hiphoto' p117 Yulia Kozlova; Brent Hofacker; Mariemily Photos; Univega; kazoka; showcake; Shahril KHMD; p118 CatMicroStock; PIMPUN TAWAKOON; p120 Paul D. Van Hoy II / age footstock; Timolina; Anetlanda; ffolas; ffolas; Magone; margouillat photo; vanillaechoes; p121 bluedog studio; CKP1001; mihmihmal; Liliya Kandrashevich; p122 KaKrue; p124 ffolas; p126 MaKo-studio; Amarita; oksana2010; sara35mm; Macrovector; p128 Stepanel Photography; Stolyevych Yuliya; Nataliya Arzamasova; asife; Ian Good; Nataliya Aarzamasova; Stolyevych Yuliya; Mshev; nexus 7; p129 Silvija Mudeniece; Kriangx1234; Lestodd; p130 cobraphotography; p132 Africa Studio; MaraZe; Elena Trukhina; ssatlva78; Bethan Jones; p133 anat chant; JoLin; zkruger; Paul Cowan; p134 solar22; p135 warat42; Moving Moment; foodonwhite; Vasily Kovalev; p136 Photosiber; Billion Photos; igorestevanovic; p137 Sanit Fuangnakhon; vvoe; abimages; p138 Jne Valokuvaus; karinrin; casanisa; simonidadj; Chalermsak; p140 alexkich